In the Weesome Hours

Maxine Vozza
Apr. 20 2016

In the Weesome Hours
1843-1889

by Mary Lackey Williams
Edited by Dianne Wehrs Vezza

ORANGE FRAZER PRESS
Wilmington, Ohio USA

1998

ISBN 1-882203-23-2
Copyright ©1998 by Dianne Wehrs Vezza

Cover Design Watercolor, Carrie Williams Lafferty, granddaughter of the poet. Painted by Poveda, Y Juan (Vicente). Italian born in Petrell in Valercia, 1857. Owner, Dianne Vezza.

Additional copies of In the Weesome Hours or other Orange Frazer Press publications may be ordered directly from:

Orange Frazer Press, Inc.
Box 214
37 ¹/₂ West Main Street
Wilmington, Ohio 45177

Telephone 1.800.852.9332 for price and shipping information
Web Site: www.orangefrazer.com; E-mail address: editor@orangefrazer.com

Limited to 2000 copies printed

Library of Congress Cataloging-in-Publication Data
Williams, Mary Lackey, 1824–1898.
      In the weesome hours : 1843–1889 / by Mary Lackey Williams : edited by Dianne Wehrs Vezza.
            p.   cm.
      Includes bibliographical references.
      ISBN 1–882203–23–2 (alk. paper)
      1. Frontier and pioneer life--Ohio--Poetry.   2. Women--Ohio--Poetry.   I. Vezza, Dianne Wehrs. II. Title.
PS3319.W655I6   1998
811' .3--dc21

                                                98-28719
                                                CIP

DEDICATION

These pages are dedicated
to all lovers of rhyme and Poesy.
To those who can read a poem in every
blade of grass, leaflet or flower: In the sky
above us and the earth beneath our feet.
To those who acknowledge an Omnipotent
Being, as the Producer and Giver of all this
good, And also love and trust Him fully
With compliments of
The Author

Mary Lackey Williams

ACKNOWLEDGEMENTS

I am greatly indebted to the members of the Washington County Historical Society (Ohio) for their encouragement and continuous support, especially David Lenington. My alma mater, Marietta College, proved to be an excellent source for the historical research portion, especially the special collections section at the Dawes Memorial Library. I owe a tremendous debt of gratitude to Mrs. Judy Pannier who oversees the library's excellent shelf resources and special collection gifts. I also wish to thank the Marietta Area Community Computer Center for computer access, and Mr. Jerry L. Bradford for his technical assistance. — *Dianne Wehrs Vezza*

TABLE OF CONTENTS

Introduction xiii
Preface by the Author xvii

CHAPTER I
MARY'S EARLY YEARS: *1843-1853*

CHAPTER II
MARRIAGE & WAR: *1854-1864*

CHAPTER III
FAMILY & FRIENDS: *1865-1875*

CHAPTER IV
MARY'S TWILIGHT YEARS: *1876-1886*

INTRODUCTION

The author of this nineteenth century poetry collection, Mary Elizabeth Lackey Williams, began saving her work in 1843, several years after her Vermont family established a farm in Newport Township, Washington County, Ohio. Once settled in Ohio she attended a small one-room country school at Yankeeburg. This exceptional collection provides the reader with an unique opportunity to study a woman of the American Victorian Age. You will share her most private thoughts as she matures from adolescence into motherhood and then on to middle and old age.

At this time Queen Victoria reigned over England and many of her subjects feared God's power was being swept aside by technology and industry. These two powerful forces seemed to dominate the minds and daily lives of her citizens. One of her subjects, Charles Dickens, would have advised you not to visit America. A city boy, he considered America to be a dirty, muddy sea of tobacco juice, a place of poor lodgings and poorer food. Our young poet might have disagreed with him. She loved her country and knew her God. Mary was a devout Methodist, and she was as devoted to religion as she was poetry. Her work embodied the prevailing religious thought of other American poets of that time. In every sense her verse is as "conspicuously religious" as those written by Bryant, Emerson, Whittier, Longfellow, Lowell, and Whitman, for they did not "urge us to believe in God by bringing forward those various arguments: cosmological, theological, ontological, moral and historical. Of these things they will have nothing. Instead, they assumed without question that it is quite as sufficient for us, as it was for them, to fall back upon personal expression and say with Saint Paul, 'I know in whom I have believed' (Bailey 231).

Ohio and Michigan's abundant natural beauty offered this poet material beyond measure. God's most minute creation received her full attention. She wrote of ground ivy, blades of grass, summer rain, winter snow, and a sun setting upon a bold flowing river. The rolling rivers of eastern Ohio were not lined with industrial, electrical and chemical plants. Maples, sycamores and large willows filled the river's edge. The air was clean, and millions of stars were clearly visible. God was supreme; he was the magnificent author of the universe. As one year folded into the next Mary observed her world. She perceived that happiness was elusive, material possessions were not permanent, friendships were seldom true, love was fleeting, truth, if it existed, was complex, and only hope remained constant until death. Ultimately, she remained faithful to the belief that the explanation of all earthly activities would be answered in God's Heaven.

Thomas Hardy, English essayist, poet, and novelist felt it would be difficult for a woman to define her feelings in language which was chiefly made by men to express theirs. This was a man's world. Chivalry and honor prevailed; duels were fought over the slightest perceived offense. On a greater scale this unbalanced courage was visible during the War of the Rebellion. An "exaggerated aggressiveness" was part of what might be called the "cult of manliness." "Nearly every male of the Victorian era seemed infected by this cult to some degree..." (Boritt 67,68). Most men from the rank of general to private wished to taste danger, to be placed at the front, or to be first atop the crest of a hill. During these years her first husband, Henry, served the Union as a "brave volunteer." Passionate words of love filled the verses she wrote from 1861 to 1864. This extraordinary female used the language of men to brilliantly record what her eyes beheld and her heart instinctively knew.

Compiling this work was an enormous task. Mary was at least fifty-one when she began to copy her poems into a bound Reynolds Consecutive Book which was manufactured by Reynolds and Reynolds Company of Dayton, Ohio, and stamped with a patent mark dated June 22, 1875. During the past one hundred and twenty-three years the journal paper has deteriorated; it is dark brown and the edges crumble at the slightest touch. Mary randomly entered poems and songs, topics and dates were intermixed, entries were made by both pen and pencil, and penmanship varied widely in style and clarity.

I organized the dated work chronologically by month, day, and year. Subject or topic guided the placement of all undated verses. This arrangement allowed the poems to be placed in a logical pattern. When reading the Preface you will note the poet referred to several poems not found in this journal. Perhaps a second journal existed but was lost in the ensuing years. Publishing constraints have not allowed me to print the entire collection. Thirty-one songs and poems on friendship, temperance, and flower gardens are not included in this publication. Small four line verses were also excluded; they were written in idle moments.

With few exceptions all poems and songs, as well as the Preface and Dedication, have been reproduced as closely as possible to the original in form and content. All dates were positioned and typed in the style and manner in which they were written. For research purposes, journal page numbers have been included in the footnotes. Due to the condition of the paper or the penmanship some words were indecipherable, therefore, brackets have been used in these cases. Mary retained the (e) on common words when adding an (ing) ending, and in other cases a few words were clearly misspelled. This has been corrected. At times Mary deliberately drew upon poetic license to purposefully misspell some words to maintain rhythm within a verse or to emphasize a word for singing. In many of her temperance songs she elongates and ridicules the word "Alchohol" in particular.

Although Mary's poems are powerful and could easily stand alone, I decided to include related local and national events because their occurrence gave birth to the poetry and shaped the pattern of this poet's life from 1842 to 1898. Each carefully selected historical annotation best reflects the times and passions of the age. Historical additions in both the text and footnotes emphasize production, both industrial and agricultural, population, expansion, politics, emotional ties with France, lingering dislike of England, early concerns of slavery, effects of the Civil War, and existing social problems which created and perpetuated the temperance movement.

Mary readily admitted she did not wish to relive her human experience. In the Preface she revealed the desire to preserve her work stemmed from a willingness to share with you common moments of joy and pain.

"What if a demon crept after you one day or night in your loneliest solitude and said to you: 'This life, as you live it now and have lived it, you will have to live again, times without number; and there will be nothing new in it, but every pain and every joy and every thought and sigh and all the unspeakably small and great in your life must return to you, and everything in the same series and sequence - and in the same way this spider and this moonlight among the trees, and in the same way this moment and I myself...'" —Nietzsche

PREFACE BY THE AUTHOR

Most of readers skip over the Preface, yet I trust that this may meet the eyes of a few of my friends.

I would say that to these poems I have endeavored to impact both a moral and religious tone hoping that they may scatter good seed that will reap an abundant harvest.

They are wholly original, and very few have ever been in print. A half dozen or so have been published in one county paper under the signature of "Lizzie Lundie" my Nome de Plume.

Many are pictures drawn from real life – from scenes of my own or friends, whose heart histories I have been allowed to read.

Some of them have been written in the "we some hours" – seemingly something would whisper to me to write. A part of a stanza would continually ring in my ears, compelling me to rise, as sleep was impossible. Then without any effort on my part to think, they were jotted down as if I was copying from memory, and yet the words would be entirely new. Among these are *Broken Promise*, and *Grandmama's Babies*.

The sentimental portion I presume will interest the young most. And yet a few persons of mature years may find something congenial, and which may present phases in their own lives. It may bring back sweet memories, of sunny youth and its gay spring time in all that was bright & beautiful in life. As the poet expresses, ere the maples were yellow and the oaks – [erased]. To such I would say there is a healing balm for all ills, in Divine Power, through the intercession of our Lord and Savior Jesus Christ.

Yours respectfully
Mary Williams
Fife Lake Mich

In the Weesome Hours

CHAPTER I

Mary's Early Years
1843 – 1853

Mary Lackey was born in Vermont on August 10, 1824. Her father, Carlos and mother, Sylva, lived on a farm located on the shores of Lake Champlain. The lake, one of the largest in the United States, is one hundred and twenty six miles long and covers an area of one thousand five hundred square miles (Cram 291). It is described as a "beautiful sheet of water" drained by the Richelieu River, a tributary of the St. Lawrence (Steinwehr von 25,26). Mary spent her early childhood playing in and near this great body of water.

In the 1830's, Mary's father, like many Vermonters, decided to search for new farm land west of the Allegheny Mountains. He sold his farm, gathered his family on board a sloop, and sailed the waters of Lake Champlain to New York State. Once in New York the family traveled newly constructed canals and connecting rivers.

The Lackey family may have stayed months and perhaps years in various locations, therefore, the length of their western travels and the duration of time they spent searching for farm land is not known. They arrived in Lawrence Township, Washington County, Ohio, in time to be recorded on the 1839 Census (Washington County Census 1839 p83). In the 1840's, the family moved to adjacent Newport Township near the little village of Newport which is located along the banks of the Ohio River on a "rising knoll above the high water mark, and was one of the richest agricultural districts of the county" (Austin 261). An 1844 tax ledger shows Carlos purchased 40.9A. of poor hilly land: section 22, township 2, range 7, sw $^1/_4$ of sw $^1/_4$ which is located along County Road 22 (Long Run Road) approximately one mile from the Yankeeburg school house. Mary was eighteen when she wrote the poem, *A Year Ago* on April 10, 1843. The population of Washington County, Ohio, in 1840 was 20,694; the township of Newport had 1,678 inhabitants; the city of Marietta had 2,689 residents (Howe 505,506).

In 1844, Mary wrote of a boy she loved, sailing ships, and the Ohio River in these poems: *Destiny; I Wonder; My Heart is Ever Weary; Mon Chere Aime; We are not Strangers; Dreaming; Thee, Thee, Only Thee; Drifting; An Appeal*; and *Written at Sunset*.

The years 1845 and 1846 were turbulent ones. Mary left her father's home, and separated from her family. She poured out the pain of separation, without explanation, in the poem *My Native Home*. In *Love Platonic, Memory, Forgotten,* and *Hope — Left or Left Out* she expressed the loss of hope, of being forgotten, and how fate had shaped her destiny.

The year 1846 seemed to offer no relief. *Hope* the "brightest star" was dimming; unlike *Four Years Ago* Mary was without family and friends. The *Silent Love* with the "dark eyes" seemed unattainable.

Those "dancing" brown eyes belonged to Henry S. Williams, a New York State native. Henry, a machinist, lived and worked in the Cincinnati/Kentucky area (History of Noble Co. 538). He either wrote or traveled to Columbus to ask Mary for her hand in marriage this year. Mary E. Lackey and Henry S. Williams were married in Columbus on November 4, 1846. Nelson Doolittle, MG. performed the ceremony (National Archives H. S. Williams). According to prevailing Ohio law, marriages had to be held in the county where the bride resided. With Henry's commitment of love and marriage, the mood of Mary's poems changed. The following verses are perhaps the happiest and most sensual she recorded. They are *At Last, Catch the Sunshine, Penetration, Will You Love Me, Christmas,* and *Unuttered Thoughts.*

During these years Mary found time to write *Impromptu, A Poem, New England, Untitled, "Another change and we're upon", Ten Years Ago,* and *Time's Changes.* She also read one extensive work, *Harold — Last Of The Saxon Kings,* by Bulwer-Lytton, 1803-1873. Lord Lytton published this historical work in 1848. The first line begins, "Merry was the month of May in the year of our Lord 1052." Lord Edward (George Earle Lytton) Bulwer also wrote under the pseudonym of Pisistratus Caxton. He was a well known "English novelist, dramatist, poet, essayist, historian, translator, and journalist." His success once rivaled that of Charles Dickens (Harris 134). Lord Lytton was a prolific writer; his completed works are contained in thirteen volumes. Mary condensed his lengthy book into an epic poem of twenty-six verses, *Harold — A*

Poem. Lord Lytton noted in this historical novel "it was related by Palgrave," and recorded in a Waltham manuscript written fifty or sixty years after the battle that two monks followed Harold to the battlefield, offered ten marks for his body and claimed it. Two to three days later, Edith and Osgood identified the body. Harold, Last of the Saxon Kings, was buried at Waltham Abby (Lytton, Harold 190-191).

A YEAR AGO

Ah! thou hast changed since first we met
  In love's sweet dream; and now has set
Our sun; that brilliantly did glow
  With brightest hope — a year ago!

And times have changed as well as thou
  For all seems sad and silent now,
And where — ! ah where's the spirits glow
  That shone through all — a year ago?

Time cannot sure have wrought the ill,
  Only one year the days doth tell;
But something's changed yes — well I know
  From what you were — a year ago.

But still at fate we'll lightly smile
  Though sad the heart; we can beguile
The world; though the soul's so full of woe,
  And so unlike — a year ago!

We'll be content or try to be
  Though ever true is memory
To breathe a sigh to let us know
  She clings yet to — a year ago.

Newport Apr 10 1843

Journal page 13

DESTINY

I knew we must be parted
  And that it could not be
That we could be united
  Was too much bliss for me
I knew that in the future
  Apart our paths must lie
I looked for your departure
  It was our destiny.

I knew full well you loved me
  And it was sweet to know
That such a matchless treasure
  On me you could bestow
Although so wide asunder
  Apart our paths must be
Our souls will cling together
  It is our destiny.

Journal page 88

I WONDER

I wonder why you stay away!
  I wonder where you are today!
I wonder if you do remember,
    That parting scene in last September!

I wonder if you still love me?
  I wonder where you next will be!
I wonder if old Father Time
    We'll ever place your hand in mine!

Journal page 15

MY HEART IS EVER WEARY
Air: "Ten Thousand Miles Away"

My heart is weary, weary
  I am so sad to day
But since you cannot love me
  I am going so far away

Cho   Then blame me not for going
          Near you I could not stay
          Forever I'll be roaming
          "Ten thousand miles away".

For I had hoped so fondly
  You loved me fervently
God Bless and make you happy
  You will never again see me

May God shield you from harm love
  And may you never know
A love that's unrequented
  May kind Heaven save you the blow

Good by my love forever
  And for you I shall pray
And darling may you never
  Be as wretched as I to day

Journal page 117

9

MON CHERE AIME

My song now is hushed, and I can sing no longer
There is none that cares now to listen to me
My notes are all silenced, and, often I ponder
That if again ever I shall sing to thee?
You're far away darling – we're parted forever
We'll ne'er meet again, no never! no never!
Little thought we that so soon we should sever
When we last met together – *Mon Chere Aime!*

A song I sing for thee 'twas of mournful cadence
You listened and laughingly turned unto me
I hope that those words are not ominous for us
For if it should be so soon parted we'll be
O no, I replied we will wander together
Along this clear stream in fair or foul weather
And darling forever let us both endeavor
To be true to each other – *Mon Chere Aime*

We kissed and we parted to meet on the morrow
The morrow it came but I went far away
Yes that tomorrow brought with it much sorrow
And carried me from you forever to stay
No never again by that beautiful river
Along its green banks will we wander – no never!
Nor ever be singing those sweet songs together
We're parted forever – *Mon Chere Aime*

Journal page 22x

WE ARE NOT STRANGERS

We are not strangers surely
  Nor ever can be again
And love both pure and holy
  Shall our hearts e're enchain
I may be dreaming – dreaming
  Yet 'tis a happy dream
My thoughts with thee are teeming
  My bother is my theme

My bother! O my bother
  On this earthly abode
Should we ne'er meet together
  We'll keep that narrow road
We'll lead us where the angels
  Sing in that heavenly choir
Then thou shall be my brother
  And I thy sister there

Yet hope in silence whispers
  Hope on! hope on! hope ever
Perhaps sometime in future
  Thee'll meet me more to saver
Should fate then prove propitious
  This cruel absence end
Then thou will come my brother
  And be thy sisters friend

Journal page 64

DREAMING

Dreaming – dreaming, ever dreaming
  Dreaming of such a one as thee
Hoping – hoping, ever hoping
  That sometime thou dreamiest of me

Sailing! – sailing! ever sailing
  Guideless o'er life's chartered sea
Hoping – hoping, ever hoping
  That someday my guide thou'st be

Wandering – wandering, ever wandering
  Through this troubled world alone
Hoping – hoping, ever hoping
  That someday thou'll be mine own

Shining – shining, ever shining
  The lamp of truth to guide the way
Hoping – hoping, ever hoping
  To meet thee on some future day

1844

Journal page 68

THEE, THEE, ONLY THEE

Though friendship has the truant played
  And love has strayed away
While my frail *bark* with sails all shreds
  Alone must find her way.
Perhaps some kind and gentle hand
  Will 'list my guide to be
And hope is sweetly whispering
  Of thee – thee – only thee!

Thou art my bright my leading star
  'Tis thou alone, can guide
My erring *bark* o'er stormy seas
  Through life's tempestuous tide.
'Tis thou alone, and only thou
  The helm can mind for me,
And hope is whispering softly still,
  Of thee – thee – only thee!

Sept 1844

Journal page 15

DRIFTING

My *barque* is on a stormy sea
   The foaming billowst round it;
There's none to furl a sail for me
   Though danger dread surround it.
And at the helm there stands no one.
   No one, an anchor casting,
Its drifting on alone – alone –
   Alone, the billows breasting.

By stormy winds 'tis driven on.
   'Neath skies so dark and dreary;
No beacon light and all alone –
   So weary, O so weary!
The port Oh will it never find
   Nor ever reach the haven?
Oh God! is there no helping hand
   Beneath the skies of Heaven?

Speed on! my weary *bark* speed on,
   Ere storms thy frail masts shiver!
Thy sails will all be furled *anon*,
   Forever and forever!
And 'way beyond the *ether* blue
   Whose love death cannot sever,
We'll meet a Friend forever true,
   When we cross o'er the river.

Journal page 11

AN APPEAL

My *bark* is on the bounding billow
  And I am drifting with the tide
The briny waves must be my pillow
  There's none stands by the helm to guide
O would that kindly hands would hold me
  That kindly lips would softly smile
That kindly arms would but enfold me
  If only just once in a while.

Hearts of block and flint and marble
  That so many bosoms hold!
Encase me in my coffin *sable*
  And place me in the grave so cold.
It would be kinder — would be warmer,
  Hands of iron — hearts of steel!
Are there none that can subdue thee?
  Is there nought to make thee feel?

O! those eyes so cold, so pitiless,
  As I meet the're 'verted glance,
It seems to me I must be dreaming,
  My senses surely are entranced!
Oh, give me but one little kind word.
  Oh, give me but one little smile,
And to thy heart oh take me kindly,
  If only just once in a while.

Journal page 78

15

WRITTEN AT SUNSET

Sweet lovely Ohio how sad 'tis to gaze
At the last rays of daylight on thy cheeks crystal waves
It calls to remembrance the friends that are gone
Like the last parting sunbeams no more to return

I loved a fair girl but she faded away
And now neath the daises is lying to day
As I now watch the daylight sink down in the west
I think of her lying in eternal rest.

Alike the dim shadows stealing o'er the waves
We'll soon be o'er shadowed by death and the grave
Poor mortals are nothing but dust and decay
And like the sun setting we all fad away.

Sept 1844

Journal page 16

MY NATIVE HOME

My home – O my home by that silvery streamlet
   I can never forget it until life's pulse is still
Hid in the deep greenwood mong trembling leaflets
   Stands the home of my father by the clear rippling rill

There brother and sisters on long winter evenings
   Gather round the home circle, all there but one
How blest were her lot had heaven permitted
   To have dwelt with the loved ones – but Gods will be done

O home! what a volume in that word is centered
   How quickly the past is recalled to mind
That home! that dear home, where nought but love entered
   O memory thou art true, but yet so unkind!

Adieu! O adieu my father and mother!
   My brother and sisters, I bid you farewell
If in this cold world we cannot live together,
   We'll meet in a brighter forever to dwell.

                              _____1845

Journal page 36

LOVE PLATONIC

Platonic love 'twixt you and me
Yes, that was what it was to be
As if I could pass summer through
With your dear self and not love you

Those dancing eyes senses enslaved
Your tones are on my heart engraved
Did you none other charms possess
O! I could never love you less

But it has left a sting behind
Which has destroyed my peace of mind
Yet I would rather sorrow know
Than to abstain from loving so

But now you say we'll meet no more
The summer's idyl has passed o'er
And if you leave without regret
Do not ask, me you to forget

Well — say good by and let it be so
The last that I shall see of you
But in the future though apart
Your memory must enslave my heart

But in That Future up in Heaven
I'll meet you then our sins forgiven
If 'tis a sin to love you so
'Tis better then not love to know

Lower Newport   1845

Journal page 6x

MEMORY

I always, always, always knew
   That fate had written down for me
That I could never find in you
   A lasting friend – it could not be
I knew our friendship, fate would mar
   That you would go I know not where
To worship at a brighter star
   While I should stay and you not care

Yet still when I look o'er the past
   And think of all that's gone before
Of days too bright, too sweet to last
   To blissful ever to come more
It seems as though it could not be
   Yet still I know it must be so
Not I for you, or you for me
   Nought but the dream of long ago

Journal page 70

FORGOTTEN

Forgotten! yes that is the word
  Then there'll be nothing to regret
The past how idle! how obscured
  'Twere so much better to forget!

Forgotten! it were better so
  It was too bright – to sweet – to last
The sweetest flower is first to go!
  And with it memories of the past

Forgotten! yes oblivion brings
  A balm to soothe the saddest hour
Forgetfulness! ah let it cling
  Around my heart strings, with all power!

Forgotten! yes I *fain* would be!
  When 'neath the grasses I shall lie,
Not then, not then remember me!
  To drop a tear, or give a sigh.

Journal page 98

HOPE
"LEFT OR LEFT OUT"

Hope: brightest star, gleams out afar
   It shines for you — it shines for me
Only this — there is a bar
   Fruition we may never see

'Tis always gleaming shining there
   Sometimes so pale again so bright
May God help those who in Despair
   Have seen this Star set in black night!

But for my Trust in Him, I know
   That long ago I should have fell
But I trust Him, at His feet bow
   Because He doeth all things well

He is our all, He is our Guide
   The crooked places strait will make
We must bow down our haughty pride
   And all our evil ways forsake

But do the best of all we can
   We're stumbling straggling by the way
Were not Our Savior more than man
   Hope would forever flee away

At best our lives are full of strife
   Like thistle down we'll blown about
Yet all the difference is in life
   If hope be left — — or is left out.
Journal page 4

FOUR YEARS AGO

Four years ago! four years ago!
  How sad the change since that bright time
For friendship then in sweetest ties
  Bound hearts that now no more are mine
Yes vanished now those happy hours
  Those golden dreams of bygone days;
When sorrow once its blight has cast
  Joy ne'er again can shed its rays

My friends have gone and far from home
  I look around and cannot find
A single heart that cares for me
  Or care where'er my footsteps tend
Deceit and falsehood hand in hand
  With poisoned shafts and pointed darts
The indefensible deep to wound
  And tear each fiber of the heart

Ah! how unlike four years ago
  Then radiant smiles a halo shed
Around each moment as it flew
  But now – alas those days have fled!
Hush! hush my muse! Be silent now,
  And stay these useless tears, that flow!
For vain regret can ne'er recall
  Those blissful hours – four years ago.

Columbus 1846

Journal page 17

SILENT LOVE

Thou never said thou loved me – never
  Yet those dark eyes a story told
Thy lips were mute – and so we severed
  Without thy trying to unfold
That love, within thine heart, there hidden –
  My soul I'd bartered to have heard.
Was thy tongue fettered – love forbidden.
  That thou should go, without a word?

Then time space came and oblivion
  Our lives were filled with other ties
At last remembrance once more given. – – –
  Ah! what a blank on my life lies!
Oh! life is passed with pain and struggling,
  Its woes and cares around me steal
With grief oppressed – and yet by smuggling
  It 'neath smiles, the wounds conceal.

Ah who would tell the world his sorrow –
  Banded about so carelessly
As 'twould be? No, let me borrow
  From the world duplicity.
And from all eyes, O let me rather
  Hide the canker in my heart –
And should we ever meet each other,
  Deceive the world, and act a part.

————

Journal page 151

AT LAST

At last — at last the heavy cloud
That's hung for many a day —
With every pleasure to enshroud
And sunshine hide away.
A *rift* at last — after so long
And always without hope;
When unforseen the mist was gone —
The sunlight — it had broke.

The mystery, was solved — at last
The vail was rent in twain.
Once more as in days that's past
The sky was seen again.
And love was lying hidden where
He had lurked many a year;
So still he was — though always there
Not daring to appear.

When sorely pressed, he raised his head
Softly began to speak
Good by to silence, then he said
My lady — love I'll seek
Away he flew o'er hill and dale
Nor loitered by the way
Until he'd told that same old tale
He'd whispered many a day.

O Love, she cried welcome at last
How long — so long thou'st stayed [erased]
The storm has passed — the skies are clear
Distrust has fled afar
And Hope again dares to appear
Again has risen our star.
Journal page 61

CATCH THE SUNSHINE

Catch the sunshine! miss the showers!
  Things will sometimes go amiss
The hardest storms will bring sweet flowers
  Sorrow you must, to enjoy the bliss.

Catch the sunshine list it vanish!
  Make your hay then while it shines,
All vexation try to banish
  Never let it try your mind!

Catch the sunshine! it might fail you,
  When you most wish for its rays
Should misfortune e'er assail you
  Ready be for rainy days!

Catch the sunshine while it lingers!
  Do not wait till clouds o'ercast!
Handle trouble with light fingers
  And you'll gain the pearl at last!

————

Journal page 86

PENETRATION

Thou never said thou loved me yet
   I knew it all the while
I read it in thy glances bright
   And in thy witching smile
I read it in thy softened tones
   Much like sweet music fell
So well I knew thou loved me
   It was not need to tell

And not with treasures golden
   Could this silent love be bought
Not for *Golconda's* diamonds
   Would I give a single thought
Although were all unspoken
   But all the sweeter guessed
And O I felt thy love was mine
   Awhile my lips thou pressed.

Journal page 58

WILL YOU LOVE ME

Will you love me more dear than another?
  And say! will you always prove true?
But, give not the love of a brother;
  More than a sister I must be to you!

I love you with tenderest emotion
  And years have been waiting to find
One to love me with deepest devotion
  Who my heart could eternally bind!

And say will you love me forever?
  And will you ne'er wish for a change
And love me so truly that never
  Your heart to another would range?

For true love can prize but one object,
  Divided love's falsely inclined
If another your heart can hold subject,
  Then your hand it can never be mine

For your being I would fill so entirely
  That with me you always could rest
I would love you so wholly so truly
  Such devotion you could not resist

Then think not of love's being divided
  There's nothing like that 'neath the sun
That question forever decided
  Never, can we love but one!

Journal page 104

CHRISTMAS

The shadows of the leafless trees
   On hilltop where
The wind-spirits rocked themselves to sleep
   Among branches bare.

Beautiful sunlight lent a charm
   Weird like it were
The winter landscape was not warm
   Though sunshine there.

And there beneath the winter sky
   He told his love
How it was told cannot tell — for
   I could not move.

And cannot now recall the words
   That his lips passed
Spell bound I sat, but oh I heard
   The truth at last.

It seemed so like a blissful dream
   Of poetry
Benumbed I could not make it seem
   Reality.

When he implored me then to speak
   My head did bow
Could only falter — let me think
   Of Heaven now.

Glory of life I had not known
   Till it was told
And vanishing bliss was now mine own
   A million fold

More blissful — yes heaven had come
   Without *allay*
And all my senses were struck dumb
   With every joy.

Earthly ideal of happiness
   Was realized
His love! O it had come to bless —
   And it sufficed.

My streaming eyes I raised to Heaven
   God I thank Thee!
That Thou hast thus this blessing given
   At last to me.

Journal page 111,112

UNUTTERED THOUGHTS

I love to read the silent thoughts
That slumber on that heart of thine
And when once learned could not be bought
With famed Australia's golden mines
Don't ask me why I prize them so?
I could not tell were I to try
O flashing glances come and go
And melt within that dark brown eye

And then I read as in a book
With open page – and I see there
Awhile I watch each changing look
Thoughts that are holy pure and fair.
That magic glance – that mystic smile
I* silence whispers thus to me
That in that heart so free from guile
Is shrined one little thought for me.

* (n) left off by author when copying

Journal page 95

HAROLD, A POEM
Suggested by reading Bulwer's *Last of the Saxon Kings*

CHAPTER I

Alone by Luna's silver beams
  There sat a maiden fair
Upon that alabaster brow
  Rested a shade of care
The heart – the soul was not at rest
  The lips part with a sigh
The voice so softly murmuring
  O Harold wert thou nigh!

An exile and an outlaw
  O God of Heaven just!
In Thee I place my dearest hopes
  In Thee I place my trust
If 'tis thy will that he returns
  Then soon O let it be
But oh if not dear Lord of Hosts
  Soon take me Home to Thee.

Down fell the sparkling crystal drops
  And sighs fell on the air
And gentle zephyrs softly fanned
  The brow of Edith fair
A hand was on her shoulder laid
  A kiss upon her brow
A voice sighed Edith dearest
  And wherefore weepiest thou

That voice! that voice! and blushes dyed
  The cheeks of Edith's face
A manly youth stood by her side
  Was ne'er seen lovelier hair [and face?]
Dry up thy tears fair Edith
  Harold is by thy side
And here he now renews the vow
  To make thee his sweet bride

And yet thou hast a rival
  From duty I'll not swerve
That rival is our England
  I must my country serve
And when the war is ended
  And ceased her carnal strife
Then as Lady of England*
  Shall Edith be my wife.

CHAPTER II

All of the House of Godwin
  From exile had returned
Gurth, Leofwine, and Tostig
  Sweyn, and his son
Wolnoth, the mothers darling
  Harold the fathers pride
Lastly Lady of England
  King Edwards saxon bride.

*Author's note: Queen

All were received with open arms
  But Sweyn the eldest born
And of dark crimes stood accused
  And was repulsed with scorn
For he had dared in former years
  To wed a "bride of Heaven"*
Which was too great a Hierilege
  To ever be forgiven

Bare headed and barefooted
  Repentant and alone
He sought the Holy Sepulchre
  His sins there to atone
In distant lands afar from home
  His spirit took its flight
And who would ever dare to say
  It sunk in endless night

No! God is good, and God is just –
  He's promised to forgive
All that repent and turn to Him
  Through Jesus Christ may live
Though man may say your crimes are great
  To ever be forgiven
Yet when the spirit wings its flight
  Christ op's the door of Heaven.

*Author's Note: Nun

CHAPTER III

Now England dons her mourning robe
  The angel Death has come
And called away the good Monk King
  Now lords and vassals mourn
And Harold son of Godwin
  Is now crowned England's king
And shouts are heard on every side
  And makes creation ring

But hark! what dreadful sound is that!
  Comes o'er the dark blue sea!
'Tis the battle cry! a brother seeks
  A *fratricide* to be
The fierce and warlike Tostig
  Now seeks a brothers realm
Joined with the king of Norway
  Thinks saxons to o'er whelm

Vain were there hopes for terror strikes
  To each Norwegian soul
Hardrada King of Norway falls
  O'er fate he'd control
Dismayed then stood the Norsemen troops
  Hushed on the battle field,
Said England's king the day's our own
  And Norsemen now must yield

Go brother Gurth, to Tostig, on now!
　Tell him I would not slay
Go!　Save me from a brothers blood!
　And Gurth then went the way.
I come to you from Harold
　He bids you leave the field
Go back and tell my brother
　That Norsemen will not yield

His blood then be on his own hand
　For I wash mine from the stain
On! on to duty! On! on Gurth
　Though brother should be slain!
Thy brothers corpse is yonder borne
　Said Haco son of Sweyn
Said Harold England costs me dear!
　O God forgive this sin!

CHAPTER IV

Ah Harold saxon England
　Beats in thy noble heart!
Ah Edith thou hast trusted
　And waited but to part!
Harold must wed with Aldyth
　Daughter of his foe
Ere William Duke of Normandy
　Shall seek his overthrow

Then foe becomes an ally
  What matters heart should ache
And wait to meet in Heaven
  'Tis for thy country's sake
Aldyth is not thy rival
  Though she is Harolds wife
The rival is old England
  She holds his heart – his life.

O Harold! saxon Harold!
  Said Edith pleadingly
I yield my claim to thy dear hand
  If such a thing need be
Wed ere the despoiler come
  To savage our country
My heart shall wed with England
  My soul will cling to thee.

And we shall meet in Heaven
  Beyond this tale of strife
A brighter crown awaits me
  Beyond this vale of strife
There soul again shall meet with soul
  Our bodies only part
Save our country from the foe
  Wed Aldyth, falter not

CHAPTER V

The raven shrieks the battle cry
  The ravager has come
With fire and sword is laying waste
  Every saxon home
We must drive the wily Norman
  Back across the wave
Or every breast with saxon heart
  Must fill a warriors grave

Thus spoke the good King Harold
  O falter not, but pray
To God to save our saxon homes
  From Norman foe this day.
Around him stood his barons
  And Haco son of Sweyn
With many a noble saxon
  By him young Leofwine

And Gurth his best loved brother
  Stood steadfast at his right
He to the death for England
  Would battle in the fight

On came the wily Norman
  The missiles fell around
Down came the English standard
  Blood stained upon the ground
Gurth snatched it up so bravely
  And held it up aloft
Vain Harolds invocation for
  The battle it was lost

Look up O king said Haco
　　Look up and guard thy head
They're shooting arrows in the air
　　We cannot off them ward
Down came the arrows bringing death
　　Both king and courtiers fell
Last at the standard died brave Gurth
　　Left none the tale to tell.

CHAPTER VI

Alas for Edith's trusting heart
　　The sacrifice was vain
Go Edith search the battle field!
　　Aldyth seeks not the slain
A crown she sought – A crown she won
　　It graced awhile her brow
The hand through which she gained the crown
　　Is cold and palsied now

And Edith sought and there she found
　　Harold among the slain
O fate thou art most true and kind
　　We now have met again
Wed! wed at last! she murmured
　　O Harold, clasp thy bride!
Her head she pillowed on his breast
　　And sweetly smiled and died.

The Saxon O where is he not?
The Norman he has gone
By all alas! he is forgot
As centuries roll on.
Eight hundred years has come and gone
Since these events we tell
And Victoria a Saxon queen
Doth rule o'er England well.

Journal pages 38, 40, 42, 44, 46-48

IMPROMPTU

On the heights of Cumberland
Up among the woodlands
Where a stream goes tumbling
   Down a rocky height.
Dwells a lovely maiden
There upon the mountain
By that crystal fountain
   That would your eyes delight,
If you could but see her —
Ever to be near her —
If you could but hear her
   Sing those songs so sweet.
Then you would adore her
And fall down before her
A humble subject cowers
   At her dainty feet.

'Twas thus young Guy beheld her
That moment then he loved her
And so he would have told her
   But dare not be so plain
She seemed so much above him
How could she stoop to love him!
Fairer far than Helen
   Who set a Troy in flames,
So he loved on so violent
He left his home at midnight
   To go and hear his doom
So up the mountain, trackless
He hurried through the blackness
For Luna's light was lackless
   In the blackened moon.

But came a glorious morning
The rocky heights adorning
Every leaflet shining
　　And quivering 'neath the dew
There by the silver fountain,
He waited on the mountain.
His love was all he thought on,
　　And could not be untrue,
At last the lovely maiden
Came down the pathway gliding
Her lovely face reflecting
　　In the streamlet clear
His heart almost stopped beating
He felt his breath retreating
That this life was too fleeting
　　On this terrestrial sphere

What could he do to lure her
For he did so adore her
And was so much below her
　　And yet she was so dear
So glancing at her smiling
In accents so beguiling
His love to her was telling
　　Though trembling with fear
But O I love so madly
Do not reject me sadly
For I would die most gladly
　　If love you cannot give

11

At him her brown eyes glancing
His very soul entrancing
Pulses – bounding and dancing
    I think you'd better live
And do not talk of dying
She spoke so sweetly smiling
There's no need of *repining*
    My love to you I give
We'll roam these forest over
And you shall be my lover
For I can love no other
    And so will wed with you
But cannot leave the wildwood
I lived here all since childhood
So would you be my husband
    Must wed the forest too

Journal pages 67-69

A POEM

'Twas on Muskingum's flowery bank,
   Near to a wooded glen,
I sat me down to *ruminate*
   Apart from busy men.
I thought of my sweet childhoods days,
   Gone never to return,
I thought of one long loved – but lost,
   'Twas thee my gentle one!

Dost thou remember years agone,
   When we together met,
And vowed to love forever more,
   And never to forget.
That vow was broken – thou *wert* false;
   And I was left to mourn
Over my lost and blighted hopes
   Alone! alone! alone!

Roll on! Muskingum's waves! roll on!
   I would thou wert my grave!
For where so calmly could I rest
   As 'neath thy peaceful waves!
There could I lie in death's embrace
   More true than thee – I mourn
Till on that great and glorious day
   When Christ should call me home!

                    Harmar, Ohio 1850

Journal page 19

NEW ENGLAND

Land of my birth! New England dear
   I still am true to thee!
Thou tho art cold as Alpine drear,
   Thou'st many charms for me.
Though far in stranger land I sigh
   Far from my childhood's home
I'll think of thee New England dear;
   Wherever I may roam.

My soul flies o'er thy landscapes cold
   To Champlain's limpid lake
And strays along its rocky coast
   Where fonder memories wake
Of other days – of old time friends
   Gone never to return!
Low down in yonders churchyard, there
   They're sleeping in the tomb

The old schoolhouse the play-ground there,
   The tinkling, rippling rills;
The summer short, but O how sweet!
   Along my own native hills!
And when stern winter reigned around,
   The hearts it never chilled,
Of those kind, dear New England friends,
   Whose souls with love were filled.

New England, dear New England!
 I never can forget
Though years have passed since I left thee
 Thou'st fresh in memory yet
Good by! good by! a long good by
 Thy hills no more in view
My home is here is western wilds
 ~~Once more adieu! adieu!~~*
Yet heart to thee is true.
     Harmar, Ohio, 1851.

* crossed out by author

Journal page 21

UNTITLED,
"Another change and we're upon"

Another change and we're upon
Muskingum's green and flowery banks
A few there are we claim as friends
And those few have our heart-felt-thanks
My life has been a changeful one
I would not live it o'er again
Except that of my childhood house
Upon the banks of Lake Champlain

Malta, O 1852

Journal page 26

TEN YEARS AGO

Ten years ago! ten years ago!
  Those happy joyful youthful days
O friendships! love! truth and hope!
  How brightly beamed thy sunny rays!
The future O how brilliantly it beamed
  With golden days to come!
O yes I was supremely blest
  With Brother, sisters, friends, home

Ten years ago! ten years ago!
  O time remorseless monster thou!
Where are the friends that blessed me then
  Gone where say can'st thou tell me now?
O some within the golden lands
  Others on the briny sea
But many more now sleep in death
  Gone — gone into eternity

Oh! who is such a wonder of change
  Would wish to live thus all alone
Away! away ye faces strange!
  Give one old friend to lien upon!
But all are gone! yes all are gone!
  No one! not one remains! O no!
Not one is here to call upon,
  That was my friend — Ten Years Ago!

Apr 10 1853

Journal page 28

17

TIME'S CHANGES

Times change Oh, time's change!
Yes, we can see them come
Without a sigh of deep regret
For roses that were gone.
How short the time since balmy Spring
Smiled on each leaf and flower!
Now hangs alas the Autumn leaf,
And all is shade and shower.

The flowers we cherished in the Spring
Are fading fast away
The ivy covered cottage roof
Is yielding to decay
The friends, the loved ones of our youth,
Are sleeping in the tomb
Time's changes have wrought all this ill,
And clothed our homes in gloom.

And yet the heart can bear all this
Until alas we find
Some well known voice grows harshly cold
That once was warmly kind
'Tis then the briny tear must flow
'Twer madness to restrain
Time's changes — oh, time's changes, oh!
Alas, have come again!

When those we loved and trusted once
Have promised forth forgot
Teaching us sadly that we cling
To those who loveth not
T'were better then to die! and give
The grave its kindred dust
Than live to see times bitter change
In hearts we love and trust
                Sept _____

Journal page 34

CHAPTER II

Marriage & War

1854 – 1864

An 1850 census of Newport Township, Washington County, Ohio indicated that Mary's father, Carlos, was 45, her mother, Sylva, was 42, a brother, Oscar, was 17, a sister, Henrietta A., was nine, another sister, Angela, was one. A sister Emily had not yet been born (Washington County Census. 1850.267).

On October 25, 1859, Mary's brother Oscar Leander Lackey, a cooper, age 32, married Sarah Rosanna Rightmier and moved to Brown Co., Indiana, (Wash. Co. Marriage Records Vol 3). On Christmas Eve, 1864, Mary wrote a poem for Oscar, *As the Shades of Twilight Gather.*

Henry moved his family frequently to take advantage of existing employment and business opportunities. The family first lived and worked in Kentucky and Cincinnati, Ohio. While in Kentucky, a son, Halsee D., was born April 3, 1848. A second son, Oscar, was born in Harmar, Ohio, May 14, 1850. A third son, George Henry, was delivered by Dr. W. C. Leonhart in Malta, Ohio, June 23, 1856. Henry and Mary moved to Marietta, Ohio. The 1860 city census listed Henry and Mary as 35 years old. Their real estate was valued at $300, their personal estate at $200. Halsee was twelve, Oscar was ten, George H. was four and Estella, three. Mary's younger sister, Angela, was also living in their home. Estella died shortly after this census was taken. A producing oil well was drilled at Macksburg, near the Noble County line. Henry moved on to Noble County.

During these years Mary concerned herself with children, family, and the heart secrets of her friends in: *The First Gray Hair; A Pair of Old Shoes; To A Thunderstorm; Blighted Hopes; Too Late; Come To Me In Dreams; A Dream; To My Sister; To My Brother on his wedding day;* and *To Sarah.*

Fort Sumter, South Carolina was bombarded on April 12, 1861 (Cram 264). News of the attack reached Marietta on Saturday morning, April 13th, and on Monday morning the news of President Lincoln's call for 75,000 men arrived in Marietta (Austin 33).

Fate had determined that no household would remain untouched by this rebellion. A Presidential draft calling for three years worth of men was not ignored. Henry went to either Zanesville, McConnellsville or Somerton, Ohio, to volunteer. On October 14, 1861, at 36, he was mustered into the 62nd Regiment of Ohio Volunteer Infantry, Company "I". He trained at Columbus and at Camp Goddard in Zanesville, Ohio. He was appointed 1st Sergeant, December 19, 1861, and promoted to Sergeant Major on that same day. He was promoted to 2nd Lieutenant on May 26, 1862, 1st Lieutenant on September 11, 1862, and on July 18, 1863 he was made Captain (Official Roster Company I, State of Ohio vol v 367).

In 1861, Mary wrote *Union Song*, a poem filled with pride and patriotism. In 1862, she wrote *To Henry*. Henry urged her to remember him, and she replied with *To* and *Ask Me Not*. In 1863 she penned *To My Husband* and *In My Heart* and composed new lyrics to well-known Airs. The *Temperance Song* and *Battle Cry of Temperance* were sung at assemblies and parades. In April, 1864, Mary wrote *Do They Miss Me at Home?* and *I Miss Thee at Home*. In May, she penned *Answer to Yes We Miss Thee at Home?* and in June, *Union Song* and *On to Richmond*.

The 62nd Ohio participated in the battle of Deep Bottom Run, Virginia, which raged from August 14th through the 18th. Henry S. Williams was wounded on August 16th and died on August 26, 1864, at the Chesapeake Hospital in Hampton, Virginia. He was buried at Fortress Monroe, a strategic Union base located at the entrance to Chesapeake Bay and Hampton Roads. It was known as the "Freedom Fort" by blacks escaping slavery because General Butler labled all runaways "contrabands of war" thereby assuring their freedom. Mary and the three boys mourned the loss of a loving husband and father. Mary wore black and wrote *In Memory, You Tell Me To Be Gay, As the Shades of Twilight Gather, I Knew Yes I Knew, Fate, Hidden,* and *Only a Memory*. Mary wrote *You Tell Me To Be Gay* in September, 1864; Sherman occupied Atlanta September 2nd. Mary recalled Ecclesiasticeis, Chapter 12 verse 6, "Remember your creator before the silver chord is loosed, or the golden bowl is broken."

Mary's sister, Henrietta A. Lackey, married James Dilley, October 12, 1864 (Washington County, Ohio Marriage Records).

THE FIRST GRAY HAIR

I found a gray hair on my bonny brown head
And O it speaks volumes untold
Where the brown now abundantly crowns there instead
The gray will increase twenty fold

I found a gray hair and it speaks of decay
Of a grave somewhere waiting for me
It tells me my days are gliding away
To that country of deep mystery.

I found a gray hair, but why should a dread,
Or a shiver pass *athwart* my heart
When I always knew that I'd no lease on life
Any day it might from me depart.

I found a gray hair to me it should tell
A story of pleasure untold
Of a country up There where the ransomed shall dwell
With Christ in the City of Gold.

———————

Journal page 16

SONNET
TO A PAIR OF OLD SHOES

Dear old friends, and must we part
Yet just a little longer stay
I do not care to change — dear heart
No comfort here, with you away
"New brooms" tis said "will sweep so clean"
Yet if I am allowed to choose
To you I certainly shall lean
And cling so fast — You dear old shoes!
Yes, I'm so easy with you by
My thoughts can have the freest range
New shoes I hate abominably
Yet I'm obliged to make a change
You leave me now no chance to save you
Soul and body parted — dear old shoe.

Journal page 36

SONNET
TO A THUNDER STORM

How like a silver mountain
The snowy clouds arise
Down in a crystal fountain
Come streaming from the skies
The rain drops as they patter
Against the window pane
And keep up such a clatter
We heard nought but the rain
The little birds cease singing
And hide beneath the leavs
And bugs and flies are clinging
Beneath the dripping eaves.
And all are hushed now for a time
A thunderstorm is so sublime.

Journal page 65

BLIGHTED HOPES

We met – O it was long ago
  Thy lips were wreathed in sunny smiles
Thy mind was pure as softest snow
  Thy heart was true and free from guile.

We parted – and at friendships shrine
  We knelt and vowed that absence never
Should break the chains that bound our hearts
  Thus firmly in true faith together.

We met again, in after years
  But oh how sad a change was there!
Yet still thine eye was blue as yore
  Thy brow and cheek were just as fair.

Ah yes, those eyes were just as bright
  As when we met in early youth
Thy smile and step were just as light
  But oh! the heart had lost its truth!

And hopes and joys had vanished all
  Just like a wreath of melting snow,
Oh Friendship! art thou but a name?
  And truth a vain deceitful glow?

Oh who could bear their lot of pain
  That ever is to mortals given?
Did not unclouded yet remain
  Our beaming radiant hope of Heaven?
                _____1857

Journal page 32

TOO LATE

'Twas the same glance 'twas the same voice
  A dreamy languor through
And yet with what a difference
  'Though old it seemed so new.

And once before, more earnest words
  And yet what did they mean?
'Tis actions speaks – all words are vain
  May not mean anything!

And how confused things often grow
  When in review the past
They jostle, cross each other so
  In ashes fall at last.

His words were falling on a stone
  Oh! had they come before
How rich, how fertile they had been
  But now – the time was o'er

Spring had arrived but come too late
  The buds were shriveled so
No summer warmth could bid them bloom
  Nor fragrance o'er bestow

Too late, too late–; the dead dead past
  A faint aroma shed
But blasted with untimely frost
  It lay there limp and dead.

Journal page 14

COME TO ME IN DREAMS

O come to me in dreams love!
  Alone I think of thee, love!
No other form I see, love!
  In dreams love, come to me!
  In dreams love, come to me!

I dreamed of thee on yesternight,
  Thine eyes with love were beaming bright,
My hand thou clasped with fond delight,
  In dreams love, come to me!
  In dreams love, come to me!

Fate treats us most unkindly, love!
  O hearts that did so fondly love,
Would not on earth be parted, love!
  In dreams love, come to me!
  In dreams love, come to me!

Farewell on earth forever, love!
  In heaven we ne'er sever, love!
Till we meet there together, love!
  In dreams love, come to me!
  In dreams love, come to me!

_____1858

Journal page 56

A DREAM

You came to me when starry night
  Had over all its mantle thrown;
Your presence brought to me delight
  And happier hours than years had known

You spoke, your voice each fiber thrilled
  Your hand touched mine it brought me bliss
The past came back my life was filled
  O could my heart ask more than this?

Your arm around my waist was thrown,
  We were a boy and girl again;
The past flew backwards, that had borne
  So much to me of grief and pain.

A fragment of the long ago?
  I questioned as I sought your face
Your voice was music murmuring low
  Too many years have long passed since

Across the stream I have passed o'er
  Have waited long to meet with you,
'Tis over there we'll part no more
  Remember me – I will be true!

The voice was hushed its music gone
  And quickly changed the passing scene
My slumbers broke, I was alone;
  'Twas only nothing but a dream!

Journal page 11

TO MY SISTER

Say Angela dost thou ever
  Mind the times we waived all care.
And spent such happy hours together
  Building "Castles in the air?"

O we had the fleetest ponies,
  And scoured the country every where
We flew as swiftly as the fairies,
  In that castle in the air.

We crossed the wide and blue Atlantic
  And neath Italia's skies so fair
In gondola o'er Bay of Naples
  Flew, in that "Castle in the air"

Though clouds so oft did gather o'er us
  Obscuring all our sunshine there
Yet still we saw a silver lining
  It was our castle in the air.

There is a clear and shining river
  We're nearing to its mystic shore
And when we've cross that river over
  We then shall meet to part no more

Loved ones there for us are waiting
  And Christ who went first to prepare
A home within his Father's mansion
  And we shall find our castle there

Journal page 76

TO MY BROTHER
ON HIS WEDDING DAY

Thou hast left the home circle my brother
   Another now claims thou love
She may love thee more fondly than sister
   But truer she never can prove
And O may she treat thee as kindly
   As thy sister e'er would have done
May thy home be a dwelling of sunshine
   And from it may'st thou never roam

May the shades of adversity, never
   O'er shadow thy pathway through life;
May the sunshine of Heaven beam ever
   On thee, and thy bonny young wife.
N'er wane, may the smiles of affection,
   Be tender, confiding, and true.
For she has left father, and mother
   And sisters, and home — all for you.

While sailing o'er life's troubled water,
   Your *bark* should be tossed by the gale,
With confidence breast ever billow,
   With affection unfurl each dark sail!
List the breakers, should o'er whelm thee
   The chosen the cherished thine own;
And ne'er, let the lover in husband
   Be lost, but blended in one!
          _____Oct 25 59

Journal page 52x

TO SARAH

Farewell dearest friend, and O in thy wanderings
May thy friends prove as true as thou hast to me
May the shades of adversity ne'er o'er thee hover
And Heaven's best gifts ever fall on thee.

May thy life be one day of bright cloudless sunshine
And as thy *bark* glides o'er life's tempest toss sea
May the pure hand of love dash aside every billow
And fortune prove kinder than it has to me.

And dearest sometimes when in leisure reclining
And friends throng around thee in that distant land
Think of the sad one in solitude pining
Bereft and alone, without even one friend

Then adieu! O adieu! – no more shall I meet thee
On this earth again: – but O dearest friend
Way 'yond the blue skies with love will greet thee
To part never more in Heaven's bright land.

Journal page 91

UNION SONG

Our country called her sons to save
   Her from secession's brand
My soldier went among the brave
   To help to save our land.

      My soldier went away
         To fight for liberty
      Under the spangled banner.
         The stars and stripes — the free.

To the battle field so freely went
   The bravest of the brave
He will not fear the foe to meet
   Where that spangled banner waves.

      My soldier went away
         To fight for liberty
      Under the spangled banner.
         The stars and stripes — the free.

Though the hissing shot and shell
   Shall through our armies fly
Though for him death sounds the *knell*
   For that flag he would die.

      My soldier went away
         To fight for liberty
      Under the spangled banner.
         The stars and stripes — the free.

Float on! float on ye stripes and stars
   And be forever free
But send my fighting "Son of Mars"
   Safe home again to me.

      My soldier went away
        To fight for liberty
      Under the spangled banner
        The stars and stripes – the free.

Journal page 41

TO HENRY

I am waiting husband, waiting
  As passes time so wearily
I am hoping husband, hoping
  Your return safe home to me.
Though tyrant hands would *feign* oppress us
  And enslave our free country
Stout hearts will see our wrongs all righted
  Under the banner of the free

I am waiting husband, waiting
  For the storm to pass away
I am hoping husband, hoping
  Your return fore'er to stay.
Though our flag be stained and tarnished
  With treachery – that galling brand
There's ropes enough to hang all traitors
  And no lack of willing hands.

I am waiting husband, waiting
  For the issue soon must be.
I am hoping husband, hoping
  That our homes will soon be free
On one side stands right and Heaven
  God our help will win be
Trust in Him, and He will save us
  From the curse of tyranny.
              1862

Journal page 105

TO

You tell I must not forget you
And do you think I could forget
One whose every act was kindness
Whose absence sadly I regret
Remember you, while life is left me
I will retain your memory
Thy loss of peace almost bereft me
How sad, so sad, that last adieu

Yes every vow your lips have uttered
Most sadly I remember yet
With every word my heart was fettered
I could not if I would forget.
To be in prison, and you my jailor
I would not ask a happier fate
But sad though free there to be fettered
But we will hope; and we can wait.

Journal page 65

ASK ME NOT

Ask me not why tis I love thee
   For no answer could I bring
Ask the green and tangled ivy
   Why unto the oak it clings?

You ask me if I will forget thee?
   Dost think this world will cease to move?
Or the stars cease light emitting?
   Sooner than I'll cease to love

Those dark brown eyes I see them beaming
   With every glance my heart enchanted
But 'tis so sweet to be in bondage
   A slave forever I'd remain

No ask me not, to not forget thee?
   Nor ask me not why I love thee
Could the planets cease revolving
   Around the Sun? – It could not be

———————

Journal page 60

TO MY HUSBAND

I'm thinking of the time – darling
When I stood by thy side;
And heard pronounced the magic words
That made a happy bride
My hand thou fondly pressed
And whispered soft and low
'Till death shall part us now – darling
Thou'st mine forever now.

O, yes I'm thine my darling
And still thou art so dear
As when we heard those magic words
Though passed has many a year
Yes, years into eternity –
Have rolled – tears dimmed our eyes
For a little *bud* to heaven gone
An angel 'bove the skies

1863

Journal page 55

TEMPERANCE SONG
Air: "Fellers Grave"

The banner of Temperance is now unfurled
And Intemperance that fiend of hell shall fall
Down to destruction shall quickly be hurled
It no longer shall enshroud us like a *pall*

Cho Wake drunkards wake from thy lethargic sleep
      Where Alchohol has bound thee in his chains
      We will lead thee where the mothers and children never weep
      To that *bourne* that Intemperance cannot gain

Volunteer ye wanderers – enlist in the cause
The moderate drinker also we would save
Then ere you're lost forever O quickly pause
And you fill a loathsome drunkard's grave

O ___ the briny tear of thy dear wife at home
Thy little children too must have bread
O let the glad cry be Pa sober home has come
And we'll not go supperless to bed

The banner of temperance O help to bear on
Swell the ranks of the Army of the free
Say to Old Alchohol his power has gone
That his victim no longer you will be

Cho Wake drunkards! wake from thy lethargic sleep
      Where Alchohol has bound thee in his chains
      We will lead thee where the mothers and children never weep
      To that *bourne* that Intemperance cannot gain

_____ 63

Journal page 127

BATTLE CRY OF TEMPERANCE
    Air: "Rally round the flag"
        A Parody

We will rally now for Temperance
    Rally once again
Shouting the battle cry of Temperance
    We will rally once again
    Till the victory was obtain
Shouting the battle cry of Temperance

    Chorus
Prohibition forever, hurrah! O hurrah!
Down with the wine – cup! tis Adam's ale now
We will rally now for Temperance – rally till we die
    Shouting the battle cry of Temperance.

Yes they're coming to our call now
    The noble of the land
Shouting the battle cry of Temperance
    Yes they're coming one and all now
    For Prohibition stand
Shouting the battle cry of Temperance

Prohibition forever, hurrah! O hurrah!
Down with the wine-cup! tis Adam's ale now
We will rally now for Temperance – rally till we die
    Shouting the battle cry of Temperance

Yes they're coming now in numbers
    Our name is legion now
Shouting the battle cry of Temperance
    And we will falter not
    For we've taken the vow
Shouting the battle cry of Temperance

Prohibition forever, hurrah! O hurrah!
Down with the wine – cup! tis Adam's ale now
We will rally now for Temperance – rally till we die
    Shouting the battle cry of Temperance.

We've signed the temperance pledge
    And forever will abstain
Shouting the battle cry of Temperance
    And that tempting ruby cup
    We will never taste again
Shouting the battle cry of temperance

      1863   Temperance Forever

Journal page 133

DO THEY MISS ME AT HOME?

Do they miss me at home – do thee miss me?
Do they think of the wandering one?
In thoughts do they ever caress me –
The soldier so far from his home?
Do they miss me, when at their devotions
When to God they are kneeling in prayer
And to Heaven they raise their petitions
O then! do they think of me there?

My seat at the fireside is vacant
While viewing that lone empty chair
O! do they then think of the absent
So recently met with them there?
We met – yes we met but we parted
And perhaps to ne'er meet again
O! shall I e'er meet the true hearted.
O when shall we meet to remain?

The zephyrs so softly are sighing
And gently are whispering when?
And voices me thinks are replying
Three years – three years – and then.
This war I would it was over
On wings of love swiftly I'd come
And meet again no more to sever
The loved ones so dear at sweet home!
                    April 64

Journal page 51

74

I MISS THEE AT HOME

I miss thee at home – yes I miss thee
  I miss thee when sol shineth bright
I miss thee at morn and at evening
  And at the still hour of midnight
I miss thee where ever I roameth
  I miss thee when others are near
There's none to me thy place filleth
  None other to me half as dear

Thy presence to me was sunshine
  With absence my light did depart
All pleasures to me are but moonshine
  As coldly they pull on my heart
All nature is now filled with sadness
  Silently saddened alone
My heart it can never feel gladness
  Till I meet you again at our home.

Then do not! O do not forget me!
  But sometimes pray give me a thought
I never can cease to regret thee
  The presence of others are nought
While sailing o'er life's troubled ocean
  None other my frail *bark* can guide
But alone I must breast every billow
  Till thou art again by my side
      ___Apr 64

Journal page 62

ANSWER TO
YES WE MISS THEE AT HOME?

Yes we miss thee at home yes we miss thee
The wanderer shall e'er be our care
We will call upon God to preserve thee
The soldier shall share every prayer
Distance heighten's enchantment
That ever around us was thrown
When we were blessed with the presence
Of the loved one so dear at sweet home

Love cannot be conquered by absence
Think not we will ever forget
The happiness felt in thy presence
Is clinging 'round memory yet
And never, no never! NO NEVER!
Will our love forsake the dear one
We will think of the wandered ever
Of the soldier so far from his home

Then like to a swift rushing river
And on the fast *pinions* of time
The three years will quickly pass over
Then dear one Oh cease to *repine*
Every moment will, hasten the years
Every step will diminish the distance
'Twixt home and the brave volunteer.
                    May_____64

Journal page 53

UNION SONG
"ON TO RICHMOND!"

On to Richmond! lead the way!
Forward! march without delay
And victory shall crown the day
And lay secession low
On to Richmond – traitor hearts
From loyal hands must feel the smart
For union boys will falter not
Nor e'er to traitors bow!

On to Richmond hearts so brave!
Treason then shall find a grave
For freemen never will be slaves
But ever shall be free!
On to Richmond! meet the foe!
Halt not! fear not as you go
God will help strike the blow
And give us victory.

On to Richmond! there shall wave
The spangled flag our fathers gave
When us they did from tyrants save
And gave us liberty.
On to Richmond! God and Grant
Be our watchword as we act
And Heaven will our arms direct
And bless with victory.

June 21 – 64

Journal page 55

IN MY HEART

In my heart O how I've mourned thee
   And yet my lips a silence kept
Smiles on my face. Those who have known me
   Seemed not that I in secret wept

My days have been a life of sadness
   A longing to meet thee once more
I dare not hope yet for this gladness
   Thou may'st have reached the other shore,

And yet in dreams thou comes to me
   In all the beauty of thy youth
Speaking of love – I listen to thee
   – If only it had been the truth.

But when I waken all has vanished
   And only empty air I see
The vision gone but yet not banished
   O'er flowing still my heart with thee.

———————————

Journal page 141

IN MEMORY

The brown eyes are closed and the sweet dewy breath
Too soon was cut short by the Dark Angel — Death
The cheeks that outrivaled the roses so rare
Are lying so cold in the graveyard out there.

Under the flowerets under the dew
There waiting for me, and hidden from view
Under the grapes – under the sod
The body lies resting – the spirit with God.

How careless are mortals yet often at noon
The're bright hopes all ended, and in death laid down
Then we should be ready when Jesus says come!
Then He will receive us in Mansions at Home

Journal page 25

YOU TELL ME TO BE GAY

You tell me to be gay
  For me there is no pleasure
Not even a fading ray
  Life is shorn of all its treasure
Oh no I could not smile
  Unless my heart was oaken
"The silver chord is loosed
  And the golden bowl is broken."

Way 'yond the ether blue
  Went my best earthly treasure
And now my joys are few
  With grief is filled the measure
Talk not to me of cheer
  Look at this mourning token
"The silver chord is loosed
  The golden bowl is broken."

Sept 64

Journal page 70

AS THE SHADES OF TWILIGHT GATHER

As the shades of twilight gather
I am thinking dear of you
Thinking of our parting – brother
When you bade us all adieu.

Where waves now the rebel banner
Far from kindred now you roam
But we'll not forget you brother
In your dear old northern home.

When the gathering shadows deepen
Brother I think most of you
While gazing on the starry heavens
And like those orbs I will prove true

When mist scenes of mirth I mingle
And chance to meet a suit of blue
'Tis then my thoughts in silence wander
To the battlefield – and you.

When upon the field of battle
Dost thou then remember me?
While the leaden bullets rattle
Wish thou I should think of thee?

May God in mercy grant us brother
A meeting on this earth once more
When our now *ensanguine* country
Shall no more be drenched in gore

When our bright and starry banner
  Waves from Maine to Mexico
From Atlantic to Pacific.
  A nation's blood shall cease to flow.

Christmas Eve - 64

Journal page 45

I KNEW YES I KNEW

I knew we must be parted – the future would bring
   Disappointments and sorrow to darken our way
I knew our brief happiness would fly on time's wings
   That we together never would stay.

I knew you would go to some sunnier clime
   While I in this cold world alone here would stay
I knew that such sunshine could never be mine
   To have you with me to brighten my way

I knew, yes I knew, that pitiless fate
   Had written my doom as dark as the grave
I knew that our meeting came all too late
   And that thorns and thistles our parting would pave

And I know, yes I know thus ever alone
   Through this life I must walk though the pathway be long
I know yes I know that my sighs and my moans
   Must be smothered 'neath smiles, or breathed out in song

And I know, yes I know that this pathway will end
   That some day the river I'll gladly pass o'er
I know I shall meet thee where parting ne'er end
   Just over the stream, on that beautiful shore!

Journal page 106

FATE

I've had my romance it would thrill you
   If I the story should relate
Sometimes joy, but oh! such sorrow!
   And yet I know that it was fate.

'Twas fate that paled my cheeks of roses,
   'Twas fate that dimmed mine eyes of blue
'Twas fate brought the thorns and thistles
   Yet fate though hard is ever true

'Twas fate that brought this day of darkness
   'Twas fate that brought these woes to me.
'Twas fate pursued me unrelentless
   'Twas fate that parted me from thee

'Tis fate that causes me to wander
   From place to place yet ne'er find rest
'Tis fate! and yet I often wonder
   Why fate pursues me with such zest

Will fate to me ever prove kinder?
   And happier days for us in store
Will fate, on this I often ponder,
   Bring us together evermore

Journal page 96

HIDDEN

Our star but rose, again to hide
   Behind a darker cloud;
Nor e'er again can it emerge; —
   'Tis wrapped within a shroud.

And darkness covers all, — the mists
   Obscure the way. We know not now
Which way to turn to find the *rifts,*
   Or light might come — somehow.

But not a gleam — search as we may
   'Tis darkness meets our view
No hand but God's can break the way
   And let the sunlight through.

Only through Him can hope arise
   Through Him be made a way
Through Him — and up beyond the skies
   We may find perfect day.

Journal page 39

ONLY A MEMORY

Only a memory — and yet 'tis sweeter
Than manna from the bowers of Heaven;
A summer's idyll — yet 'tis fleeter
Than dew that falls at darkling even',
    — Only a memory

When the sun in all its splendor,
Shines o'er hills and valleys fair,
Stealing drops from leaflets tender,
And flinging them upon the air
    — 'Tis only a memory

A little *bud* to us was sent
Just at the dawning of the day,
But long before the day was spent
It withered, faded, passed away,
    — Leaving but a memory

She came to us a fairy vision
In two brief summers all was told;
God called her to His bright *Elysian*
And left us here on earth, so cold,
    — Nought but a memory

He went his country's foes to vanquish,
Laid down his life among the brave;
O how our hearts were rent with anguish!
His form from us forever gone — save
    — In memory

I had a friend her love I cherished,
We worshipped each at friendships shrine,
Death kissed her brow – from earth she perished
Was wafted to that sun – bright clime
             – Sweet memory

Sometimes I to my thoughts give way
And think if mortals could forget,
Would dawn for us a happier day –
We should have nothing to regret,
             – Not even a memory

But when beyond the pale blue skies,
To part no more we meet above,
Then memory dear to us will rise
– For Heaven will last, and God is love
             – Eternally

Journal page 93,95

Editor's Note: 3rd verse: I have found no information on
birth or date of death of this child; 4th verse: their
daughter Estella who died after the June 8th,1860
Marietta Census; 5th verse: Henry; 6th verse: most
probably her childhood friend in *Written At Sunset*.

CHAPTER III

Family & Friends

1865-1875

Mary Das 40 and lonely. She expressed her thoughts in the poem, *Alone*. She did not remarry until two years and four months after Henry died. On December 20, 1866, Justice of the Peace Abraham Young married Mary E. Williams to John S. McGuire in Noble County, Ohio (National Archives, H. S. Williams). Henry's three boys now had a stepfather. Halsee was eighteen, Oscar was sixteen, and George was ten.

Henry's sons were extremely successful. Halsee D. Williams was a machinist. He acquired Oscar's foundry in Dexter City, Ohio, when Oscar left for Fife Lake, Michigan. Halsee married Asenath Webber and had one child, Henry Burton. Asenath died in 1878. Halsee then married Emma Farley. They had three children: Julia, J. W., and Frank Howard. Halsee was a class leader in the Methodist Episcopal Church, a Republican, and an Odd Fellow (History of Noble Co. 538). Halsee died in 1924. He and his son Frankie are buried near Mary in the Dexter City Cemetery, Noble County, Ohio. Frankie died in 1894, the year he was born. At age seventy, Mary wrote the poem *In Memory of Frankie*.

J. W. served as minister of the well-attended Methodist Episcopal Church in Macksburg, Ohio, Washington County (Austin 230).

In 1903, a Professor H. B. Williams of Sandusky, a former resident of Caldwell, spoke at the Annual County Teacher's Institute on education and the connection between history and geography and other subjects (Pickenpaugh 138).

The middle son, Oscar C. Williams, successfully established several businesses in the states of Michigan, Kansas, and Ohio.

"O.C. Williams, Hardware and Tinware

Mr. O.C. Williams was born and raised in Washington County. When seventeen years old, he learned the moulder's trade at Athens, Ohio, and coming to Dexter City, he built a foundry which he conducted for one year. Selling out to his brother, he went to Fife Lake, Michigan and engaged in the lumber business, came back to Dexter City, and there engaged in the tin business in the firm of Woods & Williams. While there he married [L. M. Webber on November 3, 1877] , and went to Kansas and took a homestead and timber claim and lived on it for about three years. He again returned to Ohio and from here to Fife Lake, Michigan where he engaged in the furniture and stove business, went to Caldwell, Ohio in 1883, and engaged in the Patent Right business, and afterwards in the tinware business at Dexter City.

Mr. Williams came here [Macksburg, Ohio, Washington County] in 1884 and began the hardware and tinware business where he keeps a full line of hardware, tinware, stoves, and farming implements. His tinware is of an excellent quality as he manufactures it himself. He is prepared to put up tin spouting promptly at reasonable prices.

He is also a stock holder in the oil wells of this section. He owns two profitable drilling machines, and is prepared to contract for all kinds of drilling in any part of the State. Mr. Williams is one of our most energetic business men and enjoys a liberal patronage from citizens of this part of the county. All work done by him and all articles sold are warranted to be first-class, and to give satisfaction in every particular."

— *Austin 235,236*

The youngest son, George Henry, became an engineer. In 1880, George, twenty-three years of age, was married to a Mary E. Davinbarger, age eighteen. They had one son, William E. Mary Williams lived with them; she was fifty-five years old, and divorced (Census of Noble County, 1880).

William E. died June, 1881, and Mary wrote the poem *On the Death of Willie*. George and Mary had one more child, Carrie W., born in 1883. Carrie studied in Europe where she met and married Robert C. Lafferty, international reporter and writer. While living in West Virginia and Ohio, she enjoyed reading, reciting, and entertaining in schools, opera houses, and Methodist Episcopal churches. Her program included Shakespeare's *Romeo and Juliet*, Kipling's *L'Envoi*, and Dayton, Ohio poet Paul Laurence Dunbar's *Negro Dialect Sketches* (Vezza, advertising flyer with photograph). Carrie's second husband was William S. Richardson, a Marietta, Ohio druggist.

George Henry died in 1927. George, his wife Mary E., and daughter Carrie are buried in the Valley Cemetery which is located along Route 7 between Lower Newport and Marietta, Ohio.

Sixteen months after Mary's wedding to John McGuire, a sister, Emily W. Lackey, married Ansel W. McGee on April 2, 1868 (Washington County Marriage Records).

Very few of Mary's temperance songs and poems were dated. She dated two written in 1863, and the *Altercation between Heart V Conscience* written in 1871. She also wrote: *Intemperance; Temperance Song, Air: Washington's Grave; Song, Sequel To The Gypsy's Warning; Gentle Anna; Temperance Song, Cold Water For Me; Old King Alcohol, Air: The Sexton; On the Death of Rhoderic Dhu Gambrell;* and *Stepping Stones.*

Friendships evoke many emotions; Mary was surrounded by friends. She wrote of these friendships in the poems: *Acrostic; Infatuation; Written for a Friend; To A Friend; Gilded Chains; Only as a Brother; Thou Art Wedded to Another, Written For a friend Mrs. E.P. Morgareidge; To Mrs. May Morgariedge Power, On Her Wedding Day;* and *To Margaretta.* Mary remembered her mother in two poems, *Only in the Blue Morning Glory* and *On the Death of my Mother,* written in 1875.

ALONE

O what a bitter word alone!
   But only those who know can feel it
A smile may hide a smothered groan
   The heart may mourn and yet conceal it

You cannot see the secret tear
   That often on my eyelids tremble
And know not 'neath my laugh so clear
   There lies a heart that may *dissemble*

Though from my lips falls jest and song
   Yet all the while my heart seems breaking
Through friends may gaily round me throng
   They cannot fill this void this aching

Alone I stand there seems no one
   To care where'er my footsteps wander
And not one hand to help me on
   No all have gone away up yonder

Way up beyond the shining clouds
   Apart from tears, sighs, or *repining*
Where midst the million's throngs, crowds
   Of God, they stand – bright angels shining

Some day I too, shall go up there
   Some day my wanderings will be over
Some day I'll meet the loved ones where
   No earthly cares can o'er us hover

April 10 1865

Journal page 72

IN MEMORY OF FRANKIE

They tell me that our boy is dead
   It is not so but yet,
He left our arms, away has fled
   And we cannot forget.

A little *bud* to us was given
   A little while in our care
Then God took him to bloom in Heaven
   A flower divinely fair

Sometimes I see his smiling face
   In dreams he comes to me
And none can fill our baby's place
   Or banish memory.

Our little Frankie's earnest eyes
   In fancy oft I see
But he is far above the skies
   In angel purity

Before us only has he gone
   He is not dead; but when
God sent his angel to our home
   Then Frankie went back with him

Some day we'll meet him face to face
   Some day we'll go up there
Where baby Frankie waits for us
   In robes that angels wear.

Journal page 143

ON THE DEATH OF WILLIE

Put away that empty cradle!
　　Willie has another bed
He is sleeping 'neath the grasses
　　With the blue skies overhead
Where the gentle zephyrs *wafting*
　　From the roses sweet perfume
And yet it is and is not Willie
　　For the spirit it has gone

Put away the little dresses
　　Put away the half worn shoes
And the little toeless stockings
　　And all those broken useless toys
No more we'll listen to the patter
　　Of his feet upon the stair
Willie's gone to join the angels
　　And 'tis so lonely every where

The brown eyes closed to earth forever
　　The little prattling tongue is still
The busy waxen hands are folded
　　O God 'tis hard yet 'tis thy will
Sweetly resting with our Savior
　　Who has said "Come unto me"
Willie heard and so he left us
　　For a long eternity

Do not weep my darling Mama
　You will come to me some day
Do not grieve my dearest Papa
　Willie will meet you on your way
When you come to cross the river
　That your Willie has crossed o'er
A few more days and then forever
　We'll live upon that blissful shore.

June 15 1881

Journal page 140

INTEMPERANCE

There is a monster in the land
  Drags misery in its train
And thousands in its magic hands
  Are bound and by it slain.

The sword may martial with each host
  And scatter death around
This cursed fiend will take more lives
  And deal more poisonous wounds

I knew a youth with noble aim
  And genius marked his brow
Caught in its snares plunged into vice
  Alas! where is he now

Murdered by that ruthless fiend
  And lies beneath the sod
Murdered in the bloom of youth
  His soul is with his God.

Beware then of Intemperance
  It is the dreadful foe
Touch not, taste not the ruby cup
  Of endless death and woe.

———————

Journal page 119

TEMPERANCE SONG
Air: Washington's Grave

There's a home to be found for the homeless
Where the pure crystal waters ever flow
Where the red ruby wine never sparkles
Where is found neither want, care, or woe
Where no tears fill the eyes of the children
In this blessed cold water retreat
Then come O ye worshipers of Bacchus
And taste of these pleasures so sweet
     And taste of these pleasures that's so sweet
     And taste of these pleasures that save.
     Then come O ye worshipers of Bacchus
     And taste of these pleasures that's so sweet

O'er that home is a bright banner waving
Its colors are red white and blue
Its motto "Life and Prohibition"
It's sons and its daughters are all true
They're enlisted under this banner
To defend cold water they are sworn
And they fight 'gainst the hosts of intemperance
And will fight bravely till the battle's won

O victim of Alchohol come hither
Bitter tears shall all be wiped away
No more shall your brightest hopes wither
And your night shall be turned into day
Come hither from your lost condition
And whiskey's defenders all put down
By joining in with Prohibition
Your country's salvation to crown.
       1867

Journal page 129

SONG
SEQUEL TO THE GYPSY'S WARNING

31   He has promised — I have listened
To his vows so oft with pride
He has told me — O so often
That he would make me his bride

32   Yes he promised — I believed him
But O I would that I had not
He has left me for another
And alas I am forgot.

33   Gentle tales of love beguiling
He is whispering, I can see
He is smiling sweetly smiling
Just as once he did on me

34   She is listening and believing
So on her lips the kiss is laid
He is lying and deceiving
Like me she'll surely be betrayed.

35   Gypsy O pray go and warn her
Tell her what you've told to me
Fearing lest that he should harm her
Tell her what I've told to thee

36   Tell her — tell her how you warned me
That I listened not to thee
Tell her tell her — he will scorn her
And leave her just as he has me.

37 Tell her — tell her I am dying
    That for me life's charms are o'er
    Tell her on my couch I'm lying
    Praying she'll trust him no more
38 Tell her that in youth's bright morning
    In the grove I'll soon be laid
    Had I listened to thy warning
    I had never been betrayed.

                    1870

Journal page 129

Editor's Note: Thirty verses of the *Gypsy's Warning*
are lost. If complete, this poem would have
exceeded the epic poem, *Harold*.

SONG
ALTERCATION BETWEEN HEART V CONSCIENCE

HEART
Come Conscience let us now converse
As we through life's journey advance
　　Which of them dost thou say
　　Shall go with us on our way
King Alchohol or Temperance?

O Heart if thou my advice will take
Listen to reason and common sense
　　Thou'lt let alcohol alone
　　And claim for thine own
That gentle maiden Temperance.

Why Conscience Alchohol is so gay
I think I'll give him just one chance
　　To walk along with me
　　He is better company
Than that sober maiden Temperance.

True alchohol is a jolly old lad
But that is nought in his defense
　　He will lead thee astray
　　And set snares in the way
Thou hadst better go along with Temperance.

O Conscience I can take care of myself
Yet drink, – my pleasure to enhance
　　With my *boon* companions here
　　I can wait for many a year
There is time enough yet for Temperance.

"Time cuts down all both great and small"
As steadily he does advance
  Those to Alcohol inclined
  Sooner falls thou'lt ever find
Than the followers of Temperance.

O Conscience hush! and let me alone
Till in age farther advance
  When blooming youth has gone
  And old age come on
I will settle down with Temperance

Thou may'st not live till thou'it grown old
In blooming youth thou may'st go hence
  When the appetite is formed
  For Alchohol thou'ler find
That it is too late for Temperance

Hark! dost thou hear that mournful sound
The death-bell tolling to announce
  That a blooming youth has gone
  Who with Alcohol went on
And refused to go with Temperance.

Oh Conscience! I know that thou art right
Thou'st prompted by Omnipotence.
  I'll bid Alchohol good by
  And together we'll defy
The enemies of Temperance.

_____1871

Journal pages 137,139

GENTLE ANNA

I had a home of beauty
   Down by the ocean side
'Twas there I took my Annie
   A fair and happy bride
I promised to protect her
   And ever faithful be
But I loved wine and now she sleeps
   Beneath the willow tree.

   Toll! toll the bell! toll toll at the midnight hour
   For gentle Annie my fair and faded flower
   Toll! toll the bell so sad and mournfully!
   For gentle Annie sleeps beneath the weeping willow tree!

The willow waved before our door
   And oft at eventide
It's slender branches swept us o'er
   As we sat side by side
I pictured out the future
   How happy we should be
But I loved wine and now she sleeps
   Beneath the willow tree

   Toll! toll the bell! toll toll at the midnight hour
   For gentle Annie my fair and faded flower
   Toll! toll the bell so sad and mournfully!
   For gentle Annie sleeps beneath the weeping willow tree!

One happy year and that was all
  And then the fatal glass
Was *proffered* by a *genial* friend
  I could not let it pass
The mad'ning bowl I sought it
  No longer was I free
And now my lovely Annie
  Lies neath the willow tree!

   Toll! toll the bell! toll toll at the midnight hour
   For gentle Annie my fair and faded flower
   Toll! toll the bell so sad and mournfully!
   For gentle Annie sleeps beneath the weeping willow tree!

One night I will remember
  Her pleading lips did say
O stay at home dear Henry!
  Just for tonight do stay!
Her crystal tears were falling
  But what was that to me!
I went and left her dying
  She's neath the willow tree!

   Toll! toll the bell! toll toll at the midnight hour
   For gentle Annie my fair and faded flower
   Toll! toll the bell so sad and mournfully!
   For gentle Annie sleeps beneath the weeping willow tree!

Next morn her form lay lifeless
  Hands crossed upon her breast
With the brand of Cain upon me
  For me there is no rest
We buried her so lonely
  So sad – so silently,
And, now my gentle Annie
  Lies 'neath the willow tree!

  Toll! toll the bell! toll toll at the midnight hour
  For gentle Annie my fair and faded flower
  Toll! toll the bell so sad and mournfully!
  For gentle Annie sleeps beneath the weeping willow tree!

Journal pages 126, 128

TEMPERANCE SONG
COLD WATER FOR ME

'Ye lovers of Bacchus who bow at its shrine
And *prate* of the glories of the juice of the vine
Keep your wine! keep your wine, ye pale *debauchee*
But give, O pray give the cold water to me!

You may sing of mint juleps and egg nog so rare
Of ale and cherry bounce where you drown every care
Yet I freely give all to the charmer *debauchee!*
But I hold in reserve the bright water for me!

You may drink of your whiskey your brandy & rum
And wallow in mire and be beggared at home
You are welcome to all this ye lost *debauchee!*
But give O pray give, the bright water to me!

Here's to prohibitions — true Temperance band
Long as time rolls its round may it still firmly stand
Abstain from the wine glass trembling *debauchee!*
And pledge in a cup of cold water with me!

Journal page 122

OLD KING ALCHOHOL
Air: The Sexton

O yes, I am Old King Alchohol!
The king and peasant come to my call
There's none so rich, nor there's none so poor
But what they'll enter within my door
When I see genius with eagle eye
To the temple of Fame aspiring high
My poisoned chalice I hand to him
And with the lost I gather him in.

The king of terrors is my friend
Within his arms I millions send
The maiden fair with the rosy blush
And sparkling eyes I've hushed in death
When her ruby lips touched the sparkling wine
I knew! — yes I knew that she would be mine!
There's none too fair to enter my fold
And I gather them in both young and old!

A little child came wandering by
And in my net I caught him so sly
I gave him the drugs of the sugared wine
Then I knew in time that he would be mine
O yes! I give cider, the beer, and the wine
A little coaxing, a little time
Then they readily come to brandy and gin
And I gather them in — I gather them in!

O yes, I'm king and lord of the land!
I rule with a firm relentless hand
There's none that I fear but Temperance
And I'll do my best to drive her hence
I'll rally my forces – stand my ground
My whiskey sellers, I'll send around
I'll fill the land with these sinks of sin
Then millions of souls, I'll gather in!

Journal page 130

ON THE DEATH
OF RHODERIC DHU GAMBRELL
EDITOR OF *SWORD AND SHIELD* OF JACKSON, MISS.

Now drape in black the "Sword and Shield"
    Quenched is its brightest light
But, from the ashes of the dead
    Shall rise an orb so bright
To lead us on – thousands shall rise
    In armies shall they come
This act but stronger makes our cause
    We feel it nearly won.

        Toll toll the bell – for Gambrell he has gone
        Drape in black the "Sword and Shield"
        And bear the banner on
        And by his murdered corpse there kneel
        And swear his grave upon
        The temperance cause to never yield
        Till Prohibitions's won –

And none but cowards in the dark
    And those who fear the day
An indefenseless man would strike
    And take his life away.
Heroic courage well they knew
    Dwelt in his noble soul
They dare not face him in the day
    But night would cover all

Toll toll the bell — for Gambrell he has gone
Drape in black the "Sword and Shield"
And bear the banner on
And by his murdered corpse there kneel
And swear his grave upon
The temperance cause to never yield
Till Prohibition's won —

A martyr to the cause of God
   In brightest manhood fell
So brave — so promising, so good
   And by the fiends of hell
Yes murdered by the whiskey ring
   We cannot call them men
Fools that ere long will reach sing sing
   Or high as *Haman* — — hang

Toll toll the bell — for Gambrell he has gone
Drape in black the "Sword and Shield"
And bear the banner on
And by his murdered corpse there kneel!
And swear his grave upon
The temperance cause to never yield
Till Prohibition's won —

Dead! in his youthful manhood — dead!
  And life promised so sweet
But the avenger lives in God
  And vengeance sure will mite.
Haddock, Northrup — Gambrell — three!
  Americans, wake up!
No legalizing *dram-shops* now
  But wipe the vile sinks out!

    Toll toll the bell — for Gambrell he has gone
    Drape in black the "Sword and Shield"
    And bear the banner on
    And by his murdered corpse there kneel!
    And swear his grave upon
    The temperance cause to never yield
    Till Prohibition's won —

Journal page 77

STEPPING STONES

Be kind, be true, be friendly, when
A helping hand you can extend;
God loves the true — the kind and then
'Tis stepping stones to a righteous end

Help those who cannot help themselves
You'll find them anywhere you go!
And smile on those who toil and *delve*
It is so much, it helps them so

Avoid dissension, broils, and strife,
Unite with Peace and Harmony;
'Twill make on earth a happier life,
And stepping stones, to a heav'n'ly

Forbear the wine with bated breath!
Lest your pathway it should pave
With stepping stones, to early death,
And sleeping in a drunkards grave.

Lift up the fallen and obscure!
God made and loved them just as well,
Will take them home as safe and sure
As you, who in your mansions dwell

And all through life should be your aim
"To scatter joy with a willing hand,
As stepping stones, to take you Home
To Jesus: in a better land

Journal page 10

ACROSTIC

Amiable you should be ever
Neglect no chance of doing good
Nor fail from virtue ne'er to sever
And do as you would others should

Hesitate if Evil prompts you
Unsafe to follow her advice
Truth to happiness will bring you
Cancel all that leads to vice
Honor then will be your station
In all the phases of your life
Never fear a lost condition
Safely follow this advice.

ANNA HUTCHINS

Journal page 25

INFATUATION
WRITTEN FOR A FRIEND

If it sin to love thee,
  Then great the crime is mine;
For love and adoration,
  Within my heart combine.
No word of love was spoken
  Yet when those eyes I met
Their magic glances told me
  What I cannot forget!

Those eyes so blue, so heavenly,
  That smile in silence given.
To hear you say – I love you!
  I'd barter hopes of Heaven.
Let frown the cold and callous,
  Hearts cannot fettered be,
And ever free and fearless,
  Mine beats alone for thee.

Like tide upon the ocean,
  Like waves upon the sea,
And just as free and fearless
  shall be my love for thee.
It mocks the worldly wise ones,
  and spurns each staid decree.
Of the cold world, and its proud ones
  And dares be true to thee.

Like to the courser bounding
  Along the desert plain,
Like to the wild winds rushing
  Over the glossy main
Like to the storm, resounding
  Far o'er the grassy *lee*
The heart is just as boundless,
  And daring to be free

Journal page 56

TO A FRIEND

Let envy shoot envenomist darts
  But never never mind
Thank God that there are some true friends
  Though others prove unkind

The ivy leaf oft times conceals
  A rotten worthless tree
The very ones that censure most
  Need watching more than thee

When we meet on the other shore
  And each unfolds their scroll
Then God will judge among we all
  Which has the fairest roll.

I'd rather take the murderer's shame
  Than those, whose envious tongues
Are scattering misery and woe
  Among the helpless ones.

But dry thy tears a brighter day
  Is coming yet for thee
A Friend there is in every way
  Who ever true will be.

And weep no more – bury the past
  With buried wrongs among
A brighter day will dawn at last
  Now clouds obscure thy sun.

Journal page 85

GILDED CHAINS

I knew that you loved me and yet
   You sought another. Still
I never blamed you. You forget
   Perhaps that true hearts never will
Change, but keep on loving still

If for a moment you forgot —
   Was to your heart ingrate
And stooped to win a golden lot,
   And let love die — calling it fate.
You will repent too late — too late!

Gold could not buy you happiness
   I knew it at the time —
Would rather in my loneliness
   Live; than have a life like thine
With gleaming gold mine only shrine.

I've heard you rave of beauty's power
   Your heart e're to retain
You have not chosen beauty's flower
   You've given happiness to gain
Only a glittering golden chain.

It will prove fetters by and by,
   Bonds that you cannot break,
For, "what might been" you then will sigh
   And vainly mourn your bitter fate
But it will be too late — too late!

Journal page 5x

THOU ART WEDDED TO ANOTHER
Written for a friend Mrs. E. P. Morgareidge

Thou are wedded to another
  And my heart is breaking nigh
Every feeling I must smother
  When we meet pass coldly by
Must we meet as strangers always
  On this earth e'er parted be
Heaven will smile on us sometime
  And thou once more be all to me

Hope is whispering of this meeting
  On earth again thou must be mine
My heart thou hast long – long been keeping
  My hand must surely yet be thine
I love thee dearest just as fondly
  As when first in youth we met
The happy hours we've passed together
  O could we ever them forget

The world I know these thoughts would censure
  But judgement rests with God alone
And 'tis so sweet this contemplation
  Some day thou must be all mine own
And then come either joy or sorrow
  While we sojourn in earthly lands
Life or death I accept it freely
  So that it cometh from thine hands

_____

Journal page 66

TO MRS. MAY MORGAREIDGE POWER
On Her Wedding Day

A checkered sea thou'st launched upon
   The sun so brightly shining
And should a cloud gather *anon*
   Look for its silver lining
The lighting's flash the midnight storm
   Like noonday rays will lighten
Kind words and smiles dispel all frowns
   The darkest hour to brighten

Yet may your bark most smoothly glide
   Each wave and gale outriding
May pure affection swell the tide
   With wisdom ever guiding
Should adverse winds then sometimes blow
   Patience and love prevailing
Will take your vessel safely through
   And set you in smooth sailing.

Not always are the skies serene
   Life's path is not all flowers
Yet how much brighter is the scene
   After an April shower
A golden haze is thrown around
   Each leaf with diamonds shining
The cloud has passed away beyond
   But left its silver lining!

———————

Journal page 94

TO MARGARETTA

There swayed the tall poplars the oaks and the maples
The sumach's red berries were blushing there too
The cottonwood towered above the broad beeches
While under the shadows the violet grew
Then blossomed the bluebell – there nodded the lily
The daises and butter-cups sparkled with dew
The dandelion smiling 'mid scenes so beguiling –
The flower, the sweetest, my darling, was you.

Those eyes of dark violet soulful and tender
Mirrored the thoughts, which thy tongue dare not tell
And yet how you loved me so well I remember
Just as if yesterday – yes just as well
We cannot forget it though years may roll over
The longer the time, is the shorter it seems
As memory brings to us the past gone forever
And makes life seem brighter to think of past scenes

But Fate was against us we clasped hands and parted
It was forever we knew then and there
So we through life's voyage go on broken hearted
A smile on our lips – in our hearts dark despair
Yet pain has a panacea – life lasts not forever
Beyond these dark shadows of darkness and gloom
Hope points to a future to bring us together
When Death shall unite us beyond the dark tomb

Journal page 147

ONLY IN THE BLUE MORNING GLORY

Deep down in the blue morning glory
   In fancy I see my lost dead
Their spirits are hovering o'er me
   So softly around me they tread
O the blue the dark blue morning glory
   Such sad thoughts it whispers to me
Of the friends who have now gone before me
   The river I must cross to see

Deep down in the blue morning glory
   I can see my childhood's dear home
Around it the hawthorn and holly
   And the wild rose emitting perfume
I can see my dear father and mother
   My brother and sisters there met
The family circle unbroken
   O, could I this ever forget

The home is so far away from me
   And scattered all o'er the world wide
Are father, brother and sisters
   But Mother, in heaven abides
Now, now, the home circle is broken –
   My mother on earth never can I see,
Only – in the blue morning glory
   Where fancy brings her back to me.

———————

Journal page 80

ON THE DEATH OF MY MOTHER

Over the river our Mother has gone
And we're drawing nearer as years roll along
Roll on fleeting moments the faster they fly
We'll meet our dear Mother, above the blue sky

Above the blue ether she sings the glad song
Then why should we grieve as the years roll along
The faster they hasten, the sooner the day
When Gods shining angels shall take us away

And when we pass over we'll see that dear face
That watched us in childhood while toiling on Earth
Roll on fleeting moments, more speedily fly!
For Mother is waiting above the blue sky!

Keep courage dear hearts the race is most run
The summer is ended and autumn comes on
The sheaves will be gathered the river we'll cross
Where Mothers watching, and waiting for us

May 4th 1875

Journal page 84

CHAPTER IV

Mary's Twilight Years
1876–1887

Mary was fifty. Death, a house guest, visited more frequently in middle age. Relatives, friends and neighbors died. They seemed to fall like leaves blown free from a branch by a winter wind. Mary remembered those she loved, and wrote *Mrs. R. B. Learn, Resting,* and *Sweet Leonore.*

On July 28, 1879, Mary E. Williams McGuire filed a petition for divorce at the Noble County Court of Common Pleas against her husband, John S. McGuire on the grounds of adultery. Three women were named and others existing were not. Mary requested to be "divorced from the said John S. McGuire, and returned to the name of Mary E. Williams and the right of his property and possessions of the same that she brought with her at the time of her marriage and that she may have such further and other relief as equity may require." She was represented by the firm of Belford & Okey.

The filed court petition indicated, "...On or about the 1st day of January 1870...at the house of E. Hunter in Olive Township...and at other times and places to the plaintiff unknown did commit adultery with one Elizabeth Hunter and at other times and places to plaintiff unknown did commit adultery with other lewd women to wit Martha Fowler and a Mrs. Sidle and others." On August 8, 1879, Noble County Sheriff, F. C. Thompson's, Deputy Isaac E. McKee delivered a summons to John McGuire.

On November 7, 1879, Mary appeared in court. John failed to appear. The judge ruled that John S. McGuire had committed adultery with the "said Elizabeth Hunter as in the said petition alleged." The marriage was dissolved and annulled. "It is therefore ordered by the Court that the said plaintiff be restored to the name of Elizabeth Williams and it is further ordered by the Court in as much as the Divorce herein was granted by reason of the said aggression of the said defendant that the said plaintiff be restored to all her lands, tenements and hereditaments not previously disposed of, and it is further ordered that the said defendant within ten days from this date pay all the costs of this proceeding herein taxed at $ and in default there of that executive issue therefore."

The court costs were listed in detail. Mary was charged five cents for each additional name added to the subpoena. She added eight names; her cost, forty cents. Each additional witness cost Mary five cents. Mary called nine, and was charged forty-five cents. Mary was charged five cents for each witness in attendance at court. She produced nine; she was charged forty-five cents. Clerk fees totaled, $8.80; sheriff fees were $12.47; and judicial fees amounted to $12.80. Court costs totaled $34.07. The attorney fees charged by Belford and Okey were not of record (Noble County Courthouse Records, Caldwell, Ohio).

Although John's first act of adultery occurred in 1870, Mary did not pursue the desperate legal redress of divorce until after the sale of her household goods and treasures. She wrote *Helpless* in 1878. The other poems *My Ship, Days of Absence, Song, My Castle* and *Our Murdered President* were not dated.

Mary spent most of her remaining years living with or near her three sons. In 1884, Mary lived with Oscar in Fife Lake, Michigan. She traveled to Ohio to visit her old childhood home in Newport Township. She stayed with friends and relatives in Sand Hill and Crooked Tree. Emotions overwhelmed her; words poured out. She wrote *Dust and Ashes, Untitled "I could not dream", Only a Sprig of Ivy!, The Old Home, To Miss Libbie Smith, To Cousin Clare, Untitled "Doris you said", Where Art Thou Tonight?, We Meet Again, Forgive Me!,* and *Your Promises.*

In *The Children We Keep* written in 1885, Mary remembered her two dead children and commented on her three remaining "unaware" sons.

In 1885 and 1886, Mary wrote continually while living in Fife Lake, Michigan. She included the natural beauty of Michigan in her poetry. Mary remembered Henry in the poems *Reminiscences, Untitled "Long ago gone", Day Dreams – Our Star,* and John in the poem *Drifting Apart.* She also wrote: *A Panorama A Smile; Who Would Forget; A Snow Storm; Written on the Death of R. O. Clark; To Mrs. R. O. Clark, On the death of her husband; The Diamond Morning of April 7, 1886; Untitled "My life has been";* and *Untitled "These hillocks."*

In 1887, songs and poems flowed from Mary's pen. Mary wrote nine songs and seven poems. Most of them were written early in 1887, from January to May. Included in these is a song written in middle December 1886, and a poem written in October 1887. Mary wrote: *As Ye Sow So Shall Ye Reap; My Mary, Air: Broken Vow; Life's Web; My Muse;* and *Impromptu.*

On February 16, 1887, at the age of sixty-three, Mary wrote *Childhood Memories* while living in Macksburg, Ohio. In this poem she recalled the old farm in "dear New England", the adventure crossing Lake Champlain, and the journey on the canals and rivers that carried her West in the 1830's.

In July, Mary traveled to the place she loved, the Ohio River valley. She attended a picnic in Belpre, Ohio, at Howe's Grove, and rode upriver on the steamer *Ida Smith.* She wrote of her experiences in: *Lonely; At Howe's Grove, July 2, 1887, At a Picnic Party; A Rift; The Ohio Valley, on the steamer Ida Smith;* and *Drop by Drop.*

The *Ida Smith* launched in Parkersburg, West Virginia, in 1884, was 111.6 feet by 17.9 feet, with a draft of 2.6 feet. She ran on the Ohio River from Raven Rock, West Virginia with a Marietta Captain, Mr. Brady Morgan, and clerk, Mr. William E. Roe. In 1887, she traveled in low water from Marietta to New Matamoras, Ohio, where she connected with the *Sawyer* bound for Wheeling, West Virginia (Way 221).

Of the following poems, only one was dated, *Cupid's Experiment.* These last poems speak of childhood, fickle love, unkept promises, and a poet friend. They are: *Love's Garland; Fickle; The Rose and the Thorn; It Might Have Been; Impromptu to Owen Meredith; Cupid's Experiment;* and *By Gone Days.*

TO MRS. R. B. LEARN
On The Death Of Her Son

The o'er clouded sun again will shine
　　And banish grief and tears
God chastens — 'tis but to refine
　　And fit us for the spheres.

Had we no pain or sorrow given
　　Nor tears to dim our eyes
We should not care for God or Heaven
　　This world would all suffice.

But as it is so full of woe
　　We place our thoughts above
Where our most precious treasures go
　　Is where we [?] our love.

And God knows best He is Allwise —
　　He takes but to restore
At Heaven's gate when you shall rise
　　You'll meet your boy once more.

A home in Heaven in mansions fair
　　When you bid earth adieu
Think of the bliss awaiting there
　　Where "Georgie" waits for you.

Journal page 63

RESTING
Air: "Whisper Softly, Mother's Dying"

I am tired dearest mother
  Let me rest a little while!
Tell me gently of our Savior,
  With your sweet and pleasant smile.
For I need your kindness,
  Mother dear it rests me so,
And I am so tired and weary.
  I must rest, before I go!

    Resting, resting, ever resting
      In my loving Savior's arms
    Freed from earth and sin so dreary
    Saved forever from all harm

When these snows shall all be melted
  Running down in silver streams
Mother I shall then be resting
  Lying in a peaceful dream
When the fragrant summer daises
  Shall put on their gala dress
I'll be resting neath the grapes
  In my last and peaceful rest

    Resting, resting, ever resting
      In my loving Savior's arms
    Freed from earth and sin so dreary
    Saved forever from all harm

Mother do you think you'll miss me?
  But you know I cannot stay
And I pray that God may bless thee
  When from thee I'm gone away
He will fill my place dear mother!
  If you only trust him well
Kiss me Mother! O our Father!
  Take me where the angels dwell!

    Resting, resting, ever resting
      In my loving Savior's arms
    Freed from earth and sin so dreary
      Saved forever from all harm

        Martin, Mich Jan 20 1878

Journal page 110

SWEET LEONORE

Gone has Leonore from this weary world away
Gone to the land where the shining angels stay
I can meet my lost love never – never – more
Thee gone away up yonder – darling sweet Leonore

    I am lonely – I am lonely
      The sweet angel I adore
    Has gone away up yonder –
      Darling sweet Leonore

Would that she was here but her I cannot see
No more those ruby lips can ever speak to me
She's lying 'neath the daisies – life's joys are o'er
And O my heart is breaking – sweet – sweet
Leonore

    I am lonely – I am lonely
      The sweet angel I adore
    Has gone away up yonder –
      Darling sweet Leonore

She has crossed o'er the river – I shall go soon
I do not care to linger now she has gone
To dwell among the angels – I long to soar
Up to her I loved so dearly – my sweet Leonore!

    I am lonely – I am lonely
      The sweet angel I adore
    Has gone away up yonder –
      Darling sweet Leonore!
             Sand Hill Ohio
             Dec 22 1879

Journal page 75

MY SHIP

My ship is on the ocean
   Has sailed for many a day
Sometimes amidst the breakers
   Yet sails persistently.
With sails all torn in tatter's
   Yet it keeps on the sea
Some day through waters trackless
   My ship will come to me.

'Tis loaded down with jewels
   From India's foreign shore
And bonny silks and marvels
   So many ships bring o'er
And when my ship has landed
   My friends shall share with me.
Ere many years have ended
   My ship will come from sea.

All o'er a storm is raging
   The winds and water roll
A dreadful warfare waging
   Almost beyond control.
My ship is long returning
   I'm waiting every day
And soon it must be coming
   From seas so far away.

Journal page 35

DAYS OF ABSENCE

These dark days of absence how bitter they are
Perhaps you regret them I never shall know
You've wandered away and wandered afar
You'll never return I know that is so

First the days then I counted they rolled into years
I watched and I waited you came not again
My cheeks have lost roundness mine eyes with tears dimmed
Though tears will not bring you – they're here all the same

You wanted to see the seven wonders you said
I hope you have found them and wiser have grown
My hair has turned silver, my roses have fled
And my spirits of brightness with them too have flown

But farewell forever – perhaps neath a mound
You now may lie covered 'mong strangers and alone
As the years now roll over sweet rest may be found
I too will soon be lying beneath the gray stone.

Journal page 29

SONG

Give me one heart that's wholly true
   And I will ask no more
I thought I had found one in you
   The illusion now is o'er
Is friendship nothing but a name?
   And love but just a glow?
Then truth may hide her head in shame,
   For all is sham and show.

Sometimes I think I meet with one
   Whom I can fully trust
Too soon alas! betrayal comes
   My trust lies in the dust!
And so it is my faith has gone
   'Tis ever just the same
There is no truth in any one
   'Tis only just a name.

Journal page 58

HELPLESS

O my household goods, and treasures!
  How I mourn your loss to day
Oft I've gazed with heart felt pleasure
  On you – – – now you've slipped away

Friends one by one have followed after
  I stand alone with none to stay
My faltering steps, yet still I loiter
  Hoping for a brighter day

Yet heavy clouds still o'er me hover
  And darker drearier grows the day
No ray of light my pathway covers
  When will the clouds be blown away

Only one pale star is gleaming
  'Tis Hope yet paling every day
And soon thou'll cease for me thy beaming
  And even hope will slip away.

Jan 1878

Journal page 82

MY CASTLE

These changes how our lives they mar
   Give me that cabin old
Thou stately mansion standing there
   Worth piles of glittering gold
Within that cabin I have dreamed,
   And built divinely fair
A lovely structure I have reared
   A castle in the air!

I've built it there a hundred times.
   Only to see it fall;
Yet all the diamonds in the mines,
   Could not have bought my halls.
   (For mens yet a)*
Nor all the gold upon the earth
   (was one so)
   Nor jewels rich and rose
   (gold could not) (such)
Could buy my dreams of ** untold worth
   My castle in the air.

O talk not of the present
   I live within the past
And memory is truly mine
   The only thing that lasts.
My home, my friends have passed away
   And I am left alone
Only waiting for the day
   When I too shall go home
*unfinished work
**author crossed out
Journal page 116

OUR MURDERED PRESIDENT

Our noble chief – our President
In manhood's prime by dastard hand
Murdered. A leaden bullet sent
By stalwart office seekers clique
O'er whelming all our land.

That any man so vile could be
To dye his hands in blood so pure
Is this a land of liberty
Where murderers stalk about so free
'Twere better to secure.

Tremble then ye whom gold has bought
Though for awhile ye may conceal.
But time will bring these things about
Cliques will disband, "murder will out"
Some one will all reveal.

Ah can our rifled country rest
While dastard hearts beat in the breast
Of those who helped to strike the blow
In concert with the fiend "Gitteau"
Who caused the hero's death?

Leave not a stone unturned to lie
Watch well the secret cliques and bands
Meet guile with guile if needs must be
To find this den of infamy
Concealed within our land.

Journal page 27
Editor's Note: The assassination of President James Garfield

DUST AND ASHES

Only dust and ashes left
  Of life's bright halo scarce a ray
Only dust and ashes left.
  Of friendship's formed in youths bright day
In distant lands I've sought new friends
  In distant lands have found a home
But always always in the end
  Would to my native land return.

Only dust and ashes left
  Of all my hopes of future bliss
Only dust and ashes left
  Of all I hoped of happiness
The friends I loved were crushed by death
  Or faithless proved and turned away
Deceit and falsehood walked by stealth
  And caused me many a bitter day

Only the dust and ashes left
  Of my sweet hopes of long ago
I've found that sorrow does not kill
  And that this world is but a show
Friendship or love we cannot trust
  They're nothing only but a name,
And truth lies struggling in the dust
  Fate only sure – remains the same!

_____Crooked Tree April 1884

Journal page 132

UNTITLED,
"I could not dream"

I could not dream in these new halls
   I live within the past
Remembrance is sweet, that never fails
   The only friend that lasts
That pile of logs upon the green
   Is dearer far to me
Than live within these halls a queen
   And drop this memory

Crooked Tree Oh 1884

Journal page 116

ONLY A SPRIG OF IVY!

'Twas only a sprig – a sprig of ground ivy!
  Yet the tears from my eyes, were falling like rain,
It carried me back to the scenes of my childhood
  Which never no never can meet me again

Long years have gone by yet still how distinctly
  This sprig of green ivy brings scenes to my view
I see rolling by me the silvery Ohio,
  Its banks of green ivy with blossoms so blue.

The hopes that I've cherished misfortune has blasted
  The friends of my childhood are scattered and gone
The dearest are sleeping beneath the tall grasses
  And gone to that *bourne* whence none return

My mother has gone passed o'er the dark river
  My father so aged afar from that home
While brother and sisters so widely dissevered
  And I among strangers, alone, all alone! –

O times long ago, my heart's lost its freshness
  'Mong my "bonny brown hair" you'll find silver there
My once buoyant step has lost all its lightness
  Mine eyes have grown dim with the tears I have shed!

Yet only a sprig of trailing ground ivy
  Has spoken to me of the old long ago –
Happily for us we cannot see the future
  Which we in youth are so anxious to know
                    _____May 18th 1884
Journal page 152

THE OLD HOME

Once more upon my childhood's home
  With tearful eyes I gaze
O for one hour of times that's gone
  With friends of other days!
Strangers are now within this home
  And changes everywhere
There's scarce a feature left to tell
  That home was ever here.

The honeysuckle trampled down,
  The summer house destroyed,
And everything I see creates,
  Within my heart a void.
The showy lilies all are gone,
  The roses bloom no more,
All that is left that speaks of house
  __ The grove of Sycamores.

And father, brother, sisters, all.
  Are scattered all around,
The dearest one, our mother lies
  Beneath a grassy mound.
O change! more cruel than the grave!
  O scenes too bright to last!
O for one hour of brighter days
  Within the buried past!
                    _____ August 1884

Journal page 136

TO MISS LIBBIE SMITH

O say my dear friend, and don't you remember,
　　How careless we were in the old days of yore!
Then it was our May, but now bleak December
　　Our once sunny days, have long clouded o'er

You remember the school, our jokes and our folly.
　　The girls and the boys, our walks to and fro?
And we were so happy so gay and so jolly
　　You remember! twas many long long years ago!

You remember our parties, our games and our dances
　　Those old jolly times that can come no more
We planned out the future, and yet fickle fancy
　　Knew nothing of what was for us in store.

We parted to meet but seldom if ever
　　I sought distant lands fate decided it so,
While you more domestic old ties would not sever,
　　You remember it don't you! 'Twas years years ago!

Now once more we meet to talk old times over
　　Our eyes have grown dim, our hair turning gray
Yet our affections more true that a lover,
　　For friendship is steadfast, while love slips away.

We're walking alone toward the bright river,
　　And through the dark valley will soon wind our way
And yet while life last us, our hearts true as ever
　　Will cling to the old times, youth's sunny day.
　　　　　　　　　Sand Hill Aug 16 1884

Journal page 144

TO COUSIN CLARE

O don't you remember the old times Clare
  In the days of the old long ago
When we wandered together through the green wooded fields
  Gathering the flowers as they grew
But the woods are cut down – the flowers are gone
  The friends of our youth are laid low
While we meet together after many long years
  To talk over the old long ago!

And don't you remember in old Yankeeburg,
  The schoolhouse, that stood by the run!
Where we snowballed each other on the old hill side
  Together had oceans of fun!
But our playmates are nearly all gone away, Clare!
  Or else in the churchyard lay low
While we meet together, after many long years
  To talk over the old long ago!

And don't you remember our spelling schools, Clare
  Where together, three schools met to spell?
And don't you remember our budget of fun?
  There we had some joke to tell!
But where are the girls! and where are the boys!
  Gone where! where! answers echo
While we meet together after many long years
  To tell over this old long ago!

And don't you remember the old orchard, Clare?
  And the apples we called golden sweets?
Where many times we've stood neath its green leafy shade
  While the apples rolled down at our feet!
But the apples are gone, and the old apple tree
  Long since in the dust has lain low
While we meet together after many long years
  To tell over that old long ago.

Journal page 100

UNTITLED,
"Doris, you said"

Doris you said a hundred years
In dust we should be — but ten has passed
I've measured centuries with my tears
O will my life forever last?

Before her stood one she had loved
So many many years ago
And tenderness was in his eyes
It caused the tears from her's to flow

She held to him a dainty hand
O Lester I have dreampt sometimes
That happiness could come to me
Only to you could I resign
So by this grave our troth will plight
And as you wish so let it be
(line erased)
Through life we'll walk in Heaven's light
'T (line incomplete)

I might yet place my hand in thine
And yet I thought only in Heaven
Could such bliss e'er come to me
So by this grave our troth is given
And as you wish so let it be

Journal pages 141,142, 155

Editor's Note: Like all poets, Mary worked and reworked
verses. Some were never completed.

WHERE ART THOU TO NIGHT?

Where art thou to night, and why do I miss thee?
For the dark vail of silence has hung o'er us long
Yet often at twilight as the evening winds kiss me
I've thought of thy friendship in the long years agone.

Through misunderstanding our pathways were parted
So wandered away to forgetfulness know
But we mourned for the old days almost broken hearted
So longed for the hour of the dear long ago.

They tell me thou'rt living – perhaps I may meet thee
Again hear the music of those dulcet tones
Again as in old days with joy I may greet thee
Receive thee once more as a guest in my home.

Again as of old we may wander together
Along the old haunts as in sweet days agone
Ere all our dear friends had crossed the dark river
And left just us two, to wander alone –

The clods of the valley their faces now cover
Their lips that spoke kindness now parted from breath
Their joys and their sorrows on this earth are over
Their hearts are so still now lying in death

And out on the hill with fond memories clinging
Bereft of its treasures the home stands the same
Just as it was then when, you and I lingering
Said good by the last time – to ne'er meet again

Journal page 155

WE MEET AGAIN

We meet again, so many years
  Have passed since that glad time
I scarcely can restrain my tears
  For thoughts of "auld lang syne"
I look around and oh the change
  That meets me every where
Rude romping boys gray bearded men
  While others gone up There!

The crystal spring is just the same
  The beeches standing still
A sycamore spreads wide its arms
  There whiles a tinkling rill
A feature new is forming these
  Where finny creatures play
We never in the olden time
  Dreamed of this pleasant day

I love to think of olden times
  I love old friends the best
These olden haunts are dear to me
  Long will in memory rest
Though down in yonder cemetery
  Those that we loved now lie
Nothing is left but memory
  Of the old days gone by!

Above the broad blue firmament
   Shall meet with those dear ones
Conversing just as we do here
   Of days that's passed and gone
A few more days of strife and care
   A few more years at best
Then we shall always live up there
   In one eternal rest
            Sand Hill Aug 18th 84

Journal page 146

FORGIVE ME!

O my Darling – O forgive me!
I such bitter tears have shed
Yet my Darling how I loved thee
Even when thou deemed love dead

E'er through life it has clung & 'evined me
Bringing O, such sad regret!
Time has waned and years rolled over
But I never could forget.

O my Darling how I loved thee
When thou passed so coldly by
O my darling time's proved to me –
Love will last till life's last sigh

Around me now old memories hover
Of the days we used to meet
O! this life is almost over –
In heaven life will be complete

O my Darling – O forgive me!
I spoiled my life as well as thine
But thy coldness so deceived me
I deemed your love was never mine

But now I know when Hope lies buried
Beneath the ashes of that love
It never can be resurrected
Until we meet in worlds above

O, my Darling! – up in Heaven
Everything will be made plain
I shall know I am forgiven
For causing thee such bitter pain.

Yes my Darling – up in Heaven
These crooked places strait will be
The roughest phases be made even
Through a long eternity.

———————

Journal page 43,43x

YOUR PROMISES

You would come, you said, you know
That life for you now held a charm
And that as in the long ago
A frozen heart began to warm.
That you would seek one whom you loved
Although the world should you divide
That you had ever constant proved —
Would come, whatever should *betide*

Your promises are very like
The wind; 'Tis shifting every day
From the tropics comes so warm;
As northern breeze sweeps it away
And that is how I have found you
But yet o'er it I do not grieve,
After a storm there comes a calm
Leaving a soft and gentle breeze.

The hopes of youth I bade adieu
Over a hundred years ago
At least it seems that long to me
Since I cared how the world did go
I look above for solace now —
I have found One I can believe
His promises are all secure
I trust in Him — He can't deceive.

Journal page 71

THE CHILDREN WE KEEP

There were five of the children who came to their home
The boys counted four – of girls only one

One boy quickly from them was taken away
And saw only the light of one silvery day

The girl grew to be in years only three
Then she an angel was away called to be

While the others to manhood 'mid life and its cares
Prospered and wandered through the world unawares

Then the father was called to the children also
Who'd departed in childhood – so he had to go

Then the Boys left the home – to make homes for themselves
Their lives were all filled with their children and wives

While in a lone home the mother alone
Sits tear-stained and weary and dreams of a home

Above the blue skies – where two children bow
And await there her coming – they're all she has now
Oct 30 1885

Journal page 123

A PANORAMA A SMILE

A rippling Lake — a woody shore
Beyond are seen the emerald trees
The som're clouds are flitting o'er
The pines are waving in the breeze

A floating plank sometimes submerged
Now slowly drifts towards the shore
How much my life is like that plank
I too the sea shall cross o'er

Two little birds upon a bough
Are trilling forth their notes of love
How true they are — and what are we?
Oh! mortals are not much like thee

We off times think that we have friends
But the delusion soon is gone
For love can find no anchorage
That waves will not wash out and on

We drift along on life's dark sea
Sometimes perhaps a plank is thrown
But oftener, so mercilessly
We are left there to drift alone

Yet friendship has a balm when given
Which can dispel the fiercest storm
To take our vessel smooth and even
O'er foaming billows, free from harm.

Sometimes dismantled when we're drifting
If some kind friend were to extend
A friendly hand – the torn sails lifting
The waves would still, the storm would end

Fife Lake, Michigan July 13 85

Journal page 3

REMINISCENCES

I'm watching the bright rosy sunset,
  Thinking of the old long ago
Of a sunset 'midst blue and gold cloudlets
  'Twas just such a sunset as now
When you and I watched at the window
  Waiting for the last fading gleam
Till blue and gold blended together
  And darkness fell over the scene

The whippoorwill's song full of sadness
  So plaintively came from the grove
Soft zephyrs were stealing through shadows
  Bringing the soft notes of the dove
But never again from that forest
  Can those sweet bird-notes fall on my ear
And you too are far away dearest
  Only the gold sunset is here.

How sadly I think of that evening
  'Twas nearly the last time we met
The parting it came with the morning
  But that sunset I'll never forget
Whenever the day—god in splendor
  Is setting 'mong purple and gold
I think of that night at the window
  And the romance that never was told.

Journal page 74

157

DRIFTING APART

I know not how it is or why
But this I know that you and I
Apart are drifting; yet 'tis true
My every thought is all for you.
I know sometimes you think that I
Am wrong, at least your actions tell
Me so, And then I vainly try
To win a smile, but yet − − 'tis well;
We sometimes need a discipline
To bend our pride.
   So proud of you
I was to think that you was mine
'Till death us parted. Was it true?
Your heart has wandered, and the tie
Sometimes may severed be I fear
'Twixt you and I. Then I would die
I could not live from one so dear.

You flit about from flower to flower
And find a charm in beauty's smile
You say 'tis for the passing hour
Your idle moments to beguile.
Your idle moments! What of mine!
I scarcely know their meaning. Well,
'Tis better so, for had I time
To think I fear I might not quell
The swelling tide which will arise
Sometimes within my heart, and tells
Me, that there is something contrawise
Which you are hiding, and so
   Well:

I stop and do not dare to think
But every moment do employ; —
Then from the chain will drop a link
My mind is free from all *alloy.*

You say I seem as if all life
Was dead within me, and that you
So wonder why my actions *rife*
"All are with sadness."
                     That is true.
I never could *dissemble* when
My heart was sad all would know
That something *jarred.* Why should I then
Try to seem happy; just for show!
A remedy there is if you
Would care to find it, and to try
To cease this trifling, and be true
To me — yourself — lay falsehood by.

And yet so far apart we are,
I fear love's links are most worn out.
A blight has come our lives to mar
May be too late to change about —
Too well I know that happiness
Cannot be mine — Drifting apart
So fast as time can carry us,
We go; so blame your fickle heart.

And when we reach that other shore
We shall not meet each other there
You'll find perhaps one you love more
I shall find truth so shall not care.
                     Sept 5 1885
Journal pages 57,59

WHO WOULD FORGET?

Could I see thee once more as in youth's bright morning
Ere time had passed over and his mantle had lain
On all so enshrouding in a *pall* so alarming
To memory: that it seems it can't – be the same.

To live in remembrance me thinks it were sweeter
Too cold is reality – oft brings regret
Give memory's dreaming although it is fleeter
Than crystals on roses where the dewdrops have slept.

When kissed by the sun on a lovely June morning
The soft satin petals retaining the kiss
Could not turn away from caresses: by scorning
To meet them half way, – or refuse the caress?

So 'tis with all life, and love in the mainspring
Though cynics deride, and the stoic disclaims
Yet there is a time when remembrance comes creeping
The heart of a stoic is flesh just the same.

He will muse on the past, a tear perhaps glistening
And he hides from the world the sweet sad regret
And yet well he knows there is something still lingering
That's wound 'round his heart string – he cannot forget.

Ah! remembrance is sweet, although it brings sadness
Brings back the lost forms for whom life has set
Revives the lost tones, and almost brings madness
Yet who craves oblivion? – who would forget? —

Journal pages 113, 114

UNTITLED,
"Long ago gone"

Long ago gone now I am alone
Darling thou followed — so long ago
Thou fell for thy country and wait me anon
And soon I shall join thee and leave all below
We'll meet above the skies to never part more
With an angel between us — O blissful the thought
That Death cannot hold us — we to heaven soar
For Christ with his blood eternal life bought.

Journal page 55

Editor's Note: Estella, the "bud"; the angel.

DAY DREAMS – OUR STAR

Thou said 'twas "our Star", where in future we'd dwell
When we to this life should bid a farewell
'Thou pictured its beauties so bright and so fair
One 'most wished for death, to be wafted up there.

Thou said 'twas "our Star" – now thy spirit has gone
To explore all its mysteries and wait me *anon*
I'll find thee I'm sure when my spirit has fled
For I could not forget thee were I lying dead.

Sometimes in my musings thy presence I feel
The glad, sweet retrain of thy tones round me steal
It seems thou art saying in whispers so low
"I'm waiting my darling – I wait for thee now!"

"I'm guarding thee darling – dear heart be not sad
Soon emancipation will make thy soul glad
It will come in the Spring-time when bright roses bloom
To strew with sweet incense thy path to the tomb"

And out of that ashes, one day we'll arise
Then we'll start on our journey upward through the skies
To land in that radiance now beaming afar
That land so celestial – *Sirius* – our Star!

_____   Dec 11 - 1885

Journal page 145

Editor's Note: This is a premonition; she dies in the spring.

A SNOW STORM

Steadily, patiently, persistently came
O'er hilltop o'er forest o'er mountain & plain
Out of the gray inexhaustible gloom
The tiny snowflakes to earth to entomb

Up and down, over, out every where,
The marvelous sculptor was builded with care
Transforming things common to marvels of grace
Of splendor so dreary — yet all in its place.

Still, surely all day, and all the long night,
And all day again, the beautiful sight —
The work went on mightily — the clouds artist like
Fell back with work finished — and finished up right.

A *rift* was then opened — the bright sun looked on
The grand achievement in frost work was done.
An afternoon radiance fell over it all
On peaks, drifts, and glaziers a rose light did fall.

The great trees their branches so still without breath
With draperies so perfect, as silent as death,
Lest in fear that a breath should disturb their repose
Thus was Nature hushed just at the days close.

The world — it was muffled, the indefinite stir
Goes on 'neath earth's surface, for life is still there,
Though the earth assumes rest, and seems so asleep,
Under this stillness of snow-shapes so deep

Multiplication goes on. Neath the sun's rosy shine
Each bush had an attitude of enchantment sublime —
Of its own an expression of sudden life reared.
Spell bound in these depths bright cherubs appeared.

Tall motionless shapes like goddesses stood
In statuesque poises all over the wood.
The bent boughs made arches like granite so white,
Of marble, and silver in shadow and light.

The vistas so endless — so far down between
With figures so mystic with eye could be seen;
Haunting the galleries these statues of white
Robed in awful beauty those spirits of light.

On one side the river in bright silver light
On the other side over, a thicket in white,
When the setting sun glinted on the high rocky peaks
Where the pines and the hemlocks stood wrapped in white sheets.

Like sentinels standing 'mong the stumble shrubs low,
In grotesque disguises; too stately to bow.
Trailing and dangling and delicate vines
Wore their draperies lightly 'neath the setting sun's shine.

They bowed like veiled maidens in groups silent stood
The tall tree trunks girding to help all they could.
The oak and the ivy here stood — side by side
The ivy fast clinging like a newly made bride.

How wonderous is God — His wonderful power
Shames the cynic to silence as these mysteries tower
Above and beyond all over the sea
He rules all around Him — wrapped in mystery.

Dec 1885

Journal pages 83 - 86

WRITTEN ON THE DEATH OF R. O. CLARK

Cut off in his manhood – cut down in his bloom
And hurried away to the dark, silent tomb.
In aiding another his life it was given –
'Twill not be forgotten by Jesus in Heaven.

For Jesus so loved us, He gave up His life
For poor sinful man – this great sacrifice
That we might live, and again should arise
And ascend to our master above the blue skies.

When the Master is ready, He calls us away;
We have nought to do but serve and obey.
He had work for him up there, so took him home
To fields of *Elysian* – the bright world to come.

He was a kind father, a husband of worth
And tears in abundance have moistened the earth,
Till the trumpet shall sound – no, never again
Shall his lips speak in kindness a tender refrain

He is lost to his friends and kindred most dear;
His place none can fill – a wilderness drear
Is felt in their bosoms; such grief none can tell,
Only those whom death robs, can know this farewell.

March 1886

Who lost his life in trying to save another

Journal page 97

TO MRS. R. O. CLARK
On the death of her husband

The clouds loom up, the wild winds bluster
Thou scarcely can weather the gale.
Thy slender form bowed down with sorrow,
So hard to tread this weary vale.
"So hard, the path it is so thorny;
How can I walk it all alone!
O Lord! how long will last the midnight!
O God! how long before the morn!

The storm, it is so hard to buffet,
So drear, so dark alone to go;
O Lord how long – ere thy hand give it –
A solace to relieve this woe!"
Look up, look up and cease *repining,*
Anon will come a brighter day;
The clouds break'way – the silver lining
Shine through, to light you on your way.

Look up, look up, some One is knocking
Open the door and let Him in;
To Jesus' standard souls are flocking
Open your heart and go to Him
He only can help with your burden,
Two helpless charges look to you;
So place your trust and hope in Jesus,
And He will take you safely through.

This world is all an empty bauble,
The things of earth false to the core;
When we have all this world can give us
We sigh and wish for something more.
Nothing is solid – time destroys it,
'Twill fade away forevermore
But Heaven lasts, and time will prove it
When we shall reach that sunbright shore.

Journal page 99

THE DIAMOND MORNING
of Apr 7th 1886 ____

Away off, up the road, and over
The meadows; every bush and tree
Was hung with twinkling gems, – the clover
That in the slight wind swayed entrancingly
In tiny crashes of music so sweet.
With regal splendor touched by the sun
Ah! it was wonderous, sublime, so complete;
A work of one Creator, well done.

In crystal armor, rigid, bush and thorn
The fences were with brilliant glass veneered
The tiny twigs blushed in the rosy morn
And smiling in the rising sun was cheered
The gorgeous *tracery* of the boughs
Through interminable vistas pointed down
Resplendent – intricate it was –
A glorious beautiful diamond morn.

The field, whose summer plenitudes
Gave soft sensation to the eye
Was now an icy solitude
Of individuality
And every individual blade of grass
Stood independently arrayed
It was a glittering field of glass
That diamond morning there portrayed.

The earth was widened magnified
And the deep unmeasured blue
Seemed to dwindle 'mong these *myriads*
Of growths it over arched below.
Ah! scoffer canst thou tell to us
There is no God! – Thou knowest there is
This diamond morning testifies
None but a God could have done this.

Journal page 37

UNTITLED,
"My life has been"

My life has been spent in wandering around
From country and city to wain
Never long enough in one place to be found
To have any place seem like home
My heart ever clinging to this sacred spot
When the days of my girlhood was told
These hills may be steep, but true were the hearts
That beat in these bosoms – now cold

Nov 1886

Journal page 103

UNTITLED,
"These hillocks"

These *hillocks* are all that is left to me Clare
Of the friends whom I once loved so well
They have nearly all gone to the mansions up there
Without one single farewell.
As I read on the cold marble monuments here
In memory — each dearly loved name
I wonder who'll wet my grave with a tear
When I 'neath the grasses am lain

Journal page 103

Author's Note: To be added to the poem *After Seven Years*

AS YE SOW SO SHALL YE REAP

"As you sow, so shall you reap"
  Be careful then and sow no *tares*
Lest the weeds should choke the wheat
  And you reap a crop of tears.
        Tears of shame
        And tears of woe
You must reap just as you sow

He places good – He places ill
  You can choose it as you go
Gather up then at your will
  What it is you wish to sow
        Sow the *tares*
        And tares will grow
You must reap just what you sow

Better then to gather good
  If you wish good to bestow
Do by others as you would
  That they should do unto you
        Sow the wheat
        And wheat will grow
You will reap just what you sow

Then when Death calls by and by
  You will ready be to go
The Pearly Gates will open fly
  And you strait will enter through
        The harvest o'er
        And wheat has grown
And you have reapt just what you've sown
            Jan 27 1887
Journal page 10,11

193

MY MARY
Air: Broken Vow

I have learned to love thee, Mary
  And 'twill last through life the same
Mary! Mary! like to Byron
  "Have a passion for that name"
Dearest, thou hast made it dearer
  Every fiber of my heart
Is thrilling beating as I speak it
  Mary, we must never part!

Chorus: True to thee yes true forever
           Nor could I bear to sever
           From thee my darling never
           Thou art mine forever, ever

I shall cling to thee my Mary
  Long as life shall thrill my veins
And my tongue in loving accents
  Shall dwell upon that name
Mary! Mary! 'tis no wonder
  Poet's write it o'er and o'er
But if they had known my Mary
  Would have written of it more

No my darling! poets never
  Could one half thy virtues tell
Though upon thy name forever
  They in rhapsodies should dwell
Mary! Mary! "Blue eyed Mary!
  I love to speak thy name
Mary, should I live forever
  I shall love thee just the same
                    Feb 87

Journal page 22

LIFE'S WEB

Yes gather up the broken threads
　From out the tangled skein
And weave them in a friendly web
　That will for life remain.

Weave Love and Friendship not to break
　Should storms come on *anon*
And Truth and Trust to not forsake
　And Faith to tarry long.

Bring back the sunshine just as bright
　The moon beams on the plain
As when a child I took delight –
　And make them seem the same.

Make life to me a summer day
　With skies serenely fair
Make Love a song of ecstacy
　Sweet music in the air.

And too make me a queen of song
　Of capturous melody
So gifted that amidst the throng
　One half should bend the knee.

And make the voice that I loved best
　Come trilling back to me
As a bird returning to its nest
　From o'er the stormy sea.

So gather up the broken strands
   And tie them up again
Alas! there's many a missing link
   From out that broken chain

Now count them o'er there's Friendship who
   Promised to leave no never
A backward turn in Fortune's wheel
   And she was lost Forever.

And in her wake went Trust for she
   No longer could remain
Then Truth abashed went lingeringly
   And blushed to break the chain.

Faith closed her eyes in unshed tears
   Alas! she lay there slain
And never can that broken link
   Revive to life again

Then in the balance quivered love
   A moment – then bereft
He took his flight to realms above
   And only Hope was left.

Yes Hope the truest of them all
   Will cling while life remains
Though but a fragment should be left
   Of that once glittering chain

But one thread will not make a web
   And so our work is done
And of my *retinue* of friends
   Remains but only one

Alas! there is no web to weave
   At best 'twas spider net
A flimsy thing but to deceive
   And yet — we can't forget.

      Macksburg Feb 14 — 1887

Journal pages 101, 102

MY MUSE

My muse like a harp that is stringless & broken
And mute in the old halls where once 'twas the life
Companionless, lonely, so weird and forsaken
It hangs 'midst the cobwebs with memories ripe

Back, back among scenes of wealth and abundance
With beautiful maidens to whom love lent wings
But the maidens have vanished — the harp hangs in silence
And all its enchantment is lost with its strings.

My muse, once was joyful — friends I had so many
I scarcely could count them as "round me they hung"
One by one they have left me to cross the dark river
Or with hearts estranged a coldness has sprung.

Far better Deaths angel, the breath at once stilling
Than live in a world false to every vow
O Love! — sweetest flower an essence distilling
But falsehood's black vapor hangs over thee now.

I ask but one friend whom I can trust forever
(Whom deceit could, near take away)
One and one only with me to abide;
One whom reverses ca turn from me never
(Too constant to ever from my side to stray)
One, and one only to stand by my side.

But constancy only is found 'mong angels
The friendships of earth can count nought but dust
But there's One above us who ever is changeless
One up in Heaven, we fully can trust.

                    5   24 - 87
Journal page 109

IMPROMPTU

I'm sad to night, for I remember
  Once I had the kindest friend,
But like the green leaves in September
  Although so *verdant*, soon will end

The biting frosts of chill November
  Their life will take some dreary day,
While the cold winds of December
  Will sweep them every one away.

So it is when fortune favors
  Loving friends will cling around
Change the scene — our friends have left us
  Not a single one is found

As we pass them other objects
  Them engross — — attention claims
Ah! we have no loyal subjects
  Not a faithful one remains.

And 'tis well that come reverses —
  Thereby worth can estimate
Nought are we but dust and ashes
  Nothing worthy to elate.

And 'tis soon we find our level
  When our riches fade away
"Money is the root of evil"
  The wise have said before today.

                    Dexter City, Oct 22 - 87

Journal page 107

CHILDHOOD MEMORIES

I'm thinking of my childhood
  How many years ago
Since in the dear New England
  The parting tears did flow
For I was leaving playmates there,
  Whom I remember yet – ,
Remember looking back again
  Another glance to get.

Remember well the vessel that
  We took passage within
The shallow little cabin we
  Could not stand straight there in.
'Twas just a *sloop* that only took
  Us over Lake Champlain,
And 'midst the waves we were five days
  Ere we saw land again.

And then there was no railroad
  So we rode on the canal
Making twenty miles per day,
  And that was doing well.
Although we made but little speed
  We had a jolly time;
For passengers were comrades then
  All along the line

And we were five weeks coming
  It now would take two days
Had any one then told us
  Of such a speedy way
We would have called him loony
  Would not believe a word
For sixty miles within an hour
  Would have been too absurd.

In fancy to New England
  My vision oft takes flight
Where in the fields to ramble,
  It was so my hearts delight —
And then when came the milking time —
  The sun sunk in the west;
To watch the swallows at the barn,
  Flying to their nests.

Hunting for the hen's nests too
  All around the barn.
So high upon the scaffold
  And never meeting harm
Climbing to the swallow beam,
  Jumping to the hay
Among the fragrant clover tops,
  And the new mown hay.

Out into the pasture lot
  Down among the grass
Hunting for the strawberries
  Finding ground birds nests and
Then down to meadow brook
  Where little minnows swim
Which we caught upon a hook!
  We made out of a pin.

Out among the iris blades
  We gathered blossoms blue,
Down within the clover lot
  Was where the violets grew.
And over in the meadow field
  Were spotted lilies too
Daises white and buttercups
  All sparkling with the dew

Down to the limpid lake to row
  Within a tiny boat
Or else upon a plank we'd go
  And on the water float.
When myriad's of wild ducks came
  Swimming around in flocks
In the lake and out again
  Among the jutting rocks

Down among the cedar swamps
　　Gathering winter greens
Out among the thick rushes
　　To weave in tasty shreens
Down into the marshes wet
　　Gathering Huckleberries
Nimbly up the cherry trees
　　Gathering wild cherries.

Down into the sugar-camp
　　To drink out of a trough
Then at night to light a lamp
　　See to "sugar off".
Over the leafy orchard fly
　　Gathering summer sweets
The happy days of childhood are
　　Far the best we meet

Sometimes my thoughts the old days greet
　　I live them o'er again
The orchard with its Golden sweets
　　The silvery Champlain
Although only in yet seeming
　　It brings the past to view
I know 'tis idle dreaming but
　　My fancy makes it true.

Macksburg Feb 16 - 87

Journal pages 149,150,154

LONELY
At Howe's Grove, July 2, 1887 At a Picnic Party

'Tis always thus within a crowd
   I ever am alone
Then olden memories me enshroud
   Of happier days agone

Of loving friends who flocked around
   Were happy if I smiled
Now all have vanished few are found
   My moments to beguile

Of all the friends who once I loved
   Not one remains to me
Either estranged or neath the sod
   Lying so silently.

Time, ebbs and flows — rolls on and on
   We hope and watch and wait
Till Hope lies buried in her tomb —
   We're *feign* to call it "fate"

And yet what is it if 'tis not?
   'Tis all beyond control;
And countless millions — now forgot
   As endless ages roll;

Have hoped and watched and waited just
   As we all do today.
Have in their graves resolved to dust
   As time has passed away.

Journal page 12

A RIFT

The sun came breaking through the clouds
  It shone across my path
Once more as in the days of old
  I saw the sunlight flash.
Only a beam – then all was gone
  The clouds loomed up again
Only a gleam of its return
And it could not remain.

A bank of clouds – a *sombre* sky
  Is all that's left to me.
And like a corpse within a shroud
  The dream of memory.
It comes so cold it chills my heart
  Life's golden hopes are o'er
I saw them fade; saw them depart
  To come to me no more.

Oh! life is but an empty chain
  Of it we have no lease
It's broken strands in loose ends hang
  With every day increase.
The sun may shine, the clouds drop rain
  Or fall the feathery snow
Yet it can never be the same
  As in the long ago.

      7-5-1887

Journal page 81

THE OHIO VALLEY

Within this vale I feign would stay
So fraught with memories green
On every leaflet seems to be
A half forgotten dream.
Hills piled on hills it still remains
And this thought makes me sad
But a few scattering friends remain
With presence to make me glad.

And yet I feign would linger on
A charm is lingering still,
As on the breeze 'tis borne along
And whispering in the rill.
A smile – a flash – a dreamy strain
Of music low and sweet
Comes floating, stealing through my brain
So weird and incomplete.

O bonny days of long ago!
O happy vanished past!
Thoult ne'er return again I know
And wert too sweet to last.
Yet in my heart it is the same
I shut my eyes and see
The panorama o'er again
In blissful memory.

On the steamer *Ida Smith*
July 6-1887

Journal page 73

DROP BY DROP

The dew heavily lay on the cedars so green
All through among the graves we wandered between
The grass it was dripping with diamond drops wet
When the red morning sun looked on with regret.

A parting – a meeting of long years agone
A friendship once brilliant now faded and brown
'Twas seared by long absence – our roses were dead
The leaves of chill autumn strewn over the bed

And never again can the green branches grow
They were broken and withered with the old long ago
Beneath the dull ashes of hopes that have flown
They're smoldering in darkness bereft of all bloom

He who brings together and as often divides
Never without meaning and had qualified
The lives that had touched coincided for a length
Through experience deep and strengthened with strength

To separate now and be nothing henceforth
He who has qualified, knows what it is worth
Among all the cris-cross of our destiny
He works with a purpose – so mysteriously

7-17-87

Journal pages 88,90

LOVE'S GARLAND

Love, wove me a garland of roses so sweet
With hues of the roseate morn
With kisses my lips oft in ecstasies greet
With roses – but never a thorn.

Love, promised a letter, but Love was not true
I waited Despondency came
Time brought me no message – my love he did rue;
But oh! I remember his name.

On my heart it is written in letters so deep
From affection can never be torn
And my roses are withered – and oh! I must weep
For alas! I have found a sharp thorn.

Love promised to come, but alas! Love did not
His promises keep – so I mourn
His truth it is lost – his allegiance forgot –
And his roses are covered with thorns

Love comes not – he comes not – he has me betrayed;
He's fickle, inconstant, untrue,
I am standing alone and standing dismayed.
So I bid all life's pleasures adieu.

My muse on the willow – the willow so green
I will hang there forever and aye;
I will bid Love farewell, and never again
Will I trust him, for even a day.

                        5-20-88

Journal page 33

FICKLE

You've forgotten the hour – forgotten the day
   You promised to come, but your staying away;
My sky is obscured, dark clouds hover o'er,
   I'm waiting for sunshine it will come no more.

I look to the north I look to the east
   I look to the south then turn to the west
'Tis ever the same, 'tis both dark and drear,
   And ever will be so until you come near.

We'll never meet more it surely must be,
   Your face I am destined never to see;
That you are estranged, on me cast a blame,
   But if ever we meet, you will find me the same.

That my heart never wandered from you in the least,
   Was as true to you as the sun to the east.
When we parted I know you thought me to blame
   But if ever we meet you will find me the same.

You may seek another I presume that you will
   Your heart never constant new faces will fill
And find them you may, yet still well I know,
   They will not love as I do, it could not be so.

Journal page 1 1 2

THE ROSE & THE THORN

A rose in the garden grew graceful and fair
And standing so stately a thornbush grew there
The rose threw its petals over the thorn
And *feign* with it's beauties would have adorn

But the winds blew around and the petals fell torn
Do all the rose could, it would still be a thorn
She might *waft* her rich fragrance her buds drop the dew
But a thorn was a thorn all the way through

But the thorn blossomed out in clusters so white
Bringing bunches of apples in scarlet so bright
When the rose tried to pluck them it caught on the thorn
And took it home with her, to protect from shorn

So now till this day the thorn with the rose
Has always been living and will till the close
But this has a moral you plainly can see
A thorn's not a rose nor never will be.

Journal page 63,64

IT MIGHT HAVE BEEN

It might have been! we might have met,
   Before the blight of time came on,
It might have been 'fore hope had set
   Its star for us in darkened gloom!

It might have been! that when at last
   We met, we need not parted then
It might have been, that friendship fast
   Might held us then; it might have been!

It might have been that blighted love,
   Had not been given us by fate!
It might have been, that we should have
   Had that love, 'fore twas too late!

It might have been! It might have been
   To us like a forgotten dream
But memory clings and will I *ween*
   Through life – to dream what might have been!

Journal page 92

IMPROMPTU TO OWEN MERIDITH

I gaze upon thy picture here
Thy spirit shining through thine eyes
The soul within as angels pure
And almost ready for the skies

Sublime the lines thy hand doth pen
Such could not come from heart corrupt
And every *emending* line
My hungering spirit takes it up.

And in some far celestial sphere
In realm of poesy and rhyme
I *feign* would meet thy spirit there
And clasp thy hand in palms of mine.

I would not meet thee on this earth,
But up above in spirit climes,
Where all are of a holier birth —
Beyond the bounds of space and time.

When poets shall all congregate
Together shall their notes compare
Thou Meridith, thy palm will take!
Thy strains must win the laurel There.

As thee have won my soul down here
Yet in dreams only, would I meet
Thy dreamy spirit — but up There
With ecstasy I would thee greet.

Where soul with soul can meet so near
No earthly shell to keep apart;
Where nought is hidden — all is dear
An open page is every heart.

No mysteries There — & all is fair
As thy spirit that pervades thy rhyme
O Meridith! to claim thee There
As spirit guide — I'd life resign.

Above in realms of poesy
And higher soaring every day
Our dreamy thoughts reality
To never, never fade away

A song of never ending love
And of celestial poesy
O Meridith! in realms above
As brightest star — I would hail thee.

Journal page 158

CUPID'S EXPERIMENT

Cupid planted a bulb in my "Garden of Fate"
Called it love & nursed it with care
It quickly sprang up to a flourishing state
So promising, thrifty, and fair.

One day in the garden, a rough ruthless hand
In the dry scorching rays of the sun
Uprooted it – throwing it on the hard ground
'Till its poor little life was most gone

Cupid buried it deep 'neath the cold winter snow
To wait for the coming of Spring
To plant it again – in hopes it might grow
That poor, withered sapless dry thing.

A frail sickly shoot at last was put forth
Yet too flimsy to call it esteem
Yet we might keep it still; but what was it worth?
– So faded, so sickly, so slim.

With scarcely a leaf, and never a bud
'Twas watered with tears of regret
Revived for a moment then drooping its head
Bewildered it seemed to forget.

Too long it had lain beneath the sharp frost
Too long had awaited the Spring
It could not survive – Cupids labor was lost
But alas! he was *feign* to take wing.

And leaving behind reminiscence so dim
It was seemingly like a lost dream
Which one cannot catch, and yet it remains
An intangible ghost of "Has been".

'Neath the dead autumn leaves then bury it
deep
Let it lie there forever and aye
While over its grave let memory weep
For the <u>dead</u> <u>past</u> that's faded away.
                    7-17-1889

Journal pages 91,92,94

BY GONE DAYS

O by gone days! Sweet by gone days!
Fond memory brings me back again
To pleasant hours and rural shades
Upon the Lake Champlain
My childhood there was passed in love
Surrounded by kind hearted friends
Nor thought they care would ever come
Or those bright days could have an end

But change the scene and there we are
Upon Ohio's silvery tide
Where the woodmans axe loudly resounds
Through forests dense on every side.
And friends are here whom we hold dear
With hearts as warm as those of yore
And yet we scarcely know their worth
Till parted never to meet more.

Another change and we're upon
A silver stream Sciota fair
And here again we find new friends
And on our wayward lot to share
But here we must not stay too long
To Cincinnati let us *hie*
And in its bustling scenes forget
Our childhood's home and days gone by

And now again another change
Next on Missouri's distant shore
Where the hunter's rifle oft is heard
And the lusty red man plies his oar
And strange the faces all around
And stranger's smiles upon us beam
Away! away! we would not dwell
Longer upon this gloomy scene

Journal page 24

Mary Lackey Williams died April 3, 1898, in the Spring, as she predicted in *Day Dreams — Our Star.*

She is buried in the Dexter City Cemetery in Noble County, Ohio. A handsome gray monument of medium size and excellent quality marks her grave. A sprig of ground ivy was carved into the upper left corner of the stone.

The monument reads:

Mary E. Williams
Born Aug 10 1824
Died Apr 3 1898
wife of
Capt. H. S. Williams
who gave his life for his country
Aug 21 1864
and awaits the last trump at
Fortress Monroe

WILLIAMS

HISTORICAL REFERENCES

1820's – 1830's Vermont

In the 1820's Vermont shifted from a farm-based economy to a pastoral one. Plowed land gave way to pasture land as rich farmer's bought out poorer ones. At the same time, religious activities expanded. Revivalism brought thousands of converts into the Congregational, Baptist and Methodist churches. Whiskey sold for fifty to seventy-five cents a gallon. Vermonters consumed ten gallons per person per year.

By the 1830's emigration became a public question as thousands exited the state. The "sheep craze" extended to every corner of Vermont. Temperance societies gained strength; they transformed themselves to total abstinence societies and activity recruited "Cold Water Armies." Finally, in 1837, Vermonters suffered, as did the entire Union, a panic and financial depression.

Vermont citizens caught up in the "Western fever" were condemned by many to be committing nothing less than an act of treason. When departing Vermont, many families took an all-water route west beginning with a steamboat to Whitehall on Lake Champlain, a packet boat to Troy, New York on the Champlain canal, and another packet to Buffalo, New York on the Erie Canal (Vermont Historical Society 159,162,163,171,172,177,178,184,185).

The federal government established numerous Indian Reservations near the Missouri River. In 1831 the government moved the Seneca, Shawnee, and Ottawa tribes, in 1832 the Kickapoo, Kaskaskia, Peoria, Wea and Plankashaw tribes, in 1833 the Qwapaw tribe, in 1835 the Cherokee tribe, in 1836 the Iowa, Sac, Fox, and Chippewa tribes, in 1838 the New York Indians, and in 1840 the Miami tribe (Atlas of the Historical Geography of the United States plate 35 Indian Reservations, 1840). This relocation justified and clarified Carlos Lackey's decision to leave the hazards of the Missouri territory for the safety of Ohio, as described by the poet in the poem *By Gone Days*.

Cincinnati was bustling in 1840. Between 1840 and 1850 the city's population grew by ninety percent. Two thousand two hundred and fifty-eight Cincinnati residents were African-Americans (Cist 1851. 45,46). Products were shipped downstream to New Orleans, and sold at all points in-between. There were eight bell and brass foundries supplying "the whole valley of the Ohio and Mississippi with bells of all sizes, and of every use" (Cist 1841.240,241). Mills employed men and river power to mill pearl barley, corn, and feed. There were numerous and diverse iron factories. One tool grinding mill used one hundred grindstones this year. Each grindstone was eight inches thick and measured four feet in diameter (Cist 1841.251). Thirty-three steamboats were built in 1840 (Cist 1841.255). Canal boats carried bushels of corn, oats, coal, and 12,151,450 bushels of wheat to Cleveland. Barrels of flour, pork, whiskey and 782,033 pounds of butter produced by Cincinnati farmers and merchants floated north on the canal and then east to coastal markets. Shipments of lard, bacon, stoves, and lumber products decreased in 1840, but shipments of pig iron, and iron and nails increased extensively (Cist 1841.299). A variety of Cincinnati businesses prospered, including printers, producers of printing ink, makers of tin sheet, brass, copper ware, oil cloth, cabinets and furniture, pianos, and cigars.

The canals that carried these products to Cleveland and east to coastal markets came into being as a result of the Gallatin Report of 1808. Secretary of the Treasury, Mr. Albert Gallatin, was directed by the Senate, by resolution, to submit a national plan of internal improvements which included roads and canals. In this plan he suggested that western and eastern markets could be connected by constructing a canal system between existing rivers and lakes. With this combination in place products and passengers would easily be able to travel a mixture of rivers, lakes, and canals as far East as the Hudson River and Lake Champlain (Trevorrow 1). Congress refused to fund these projects, and individual states were left to their own devises to complete construction. The Ohio and Erie Canal was completed in

1832, and was a welcomed site to the weary traveler (Trevorrow 2). Ohio canals reached their peak in 1851. The use of these slow moving canals declined rapidly as railroad track completion rose. The final blow, to the few remaining canals in regular operation, came in 1913 in the form of a devastating flood (Trevorrow 3).

1842 – 1843

Charles Dickens began his American adventure in Boston, New York, and Baltimore. Leaving Baltimore by rail he transferred to a huge mail coach, a "barge on wheels." The coach wound through the Susquehanna River valley to Harrisburg. Pennsylvania (Dickens 54). At Harrisburg, during the pouring rain, Dickens transferred to a canal boat. Although small and cramped, the canal boat offered relief from the storm and provided individual tables for passengers. These tables were rearranged into one long single table for dining. The menu was lengthy. Dickens was served tea, coffee, bread, butter, salmon, shad, liver, steak, potatoes, pickles, ham, chops, black puddings, and sausage. This large fare made the trip to Pittsburgh less miserable and the mildew more bearable (Dickens 55).

Dickens lingered in Pittsburgh for three days. The citizens attempted to describe their city to the novelist; they compared it to Birmingham, England (Dickens 59). Dickens, an experienced traveler, spent hours at the Ohio River docks gathering information on the safest available steamboat. Steamboats were continually running aground, exploding, or colliding with other boats. The river was filled with hazards. Navigating was difficult, and some captains were far more gifted and talented than others. After thoughtful examination, Dickens boarded the steamer *Messenger* in Pittsburgh and continued his American adventure. He briefly stopped in Marietta, Ohio. His boat docked at Third and Ohio streets. Three days later in April, 1842, he arrived in Cincinnati, Ohio. He found Cincinnati to be a "beautiful city; cheerful, thriving, and animated." He arrived in time to view "several thousand" parading men. The Washington Auxiliary Temperance Societies were holding a convention (Dickens 61). Dickens dedicated the *American Notes* "To those Friends of Mine in

America who, giving me a welcome I must ever gratefully and proudly remember, Left My judgement FREE; and who, loving their country, can bear the truth, when it is told good-humouredly, and in a kind spirit."

The last remaining Ohio Indian tribe, the Wyandottes, sold their land and moved West this year (O'Bryant 16).

John Tyler was serving as the tenth President of the United States in April, 1842. Ohio Governor Thomas Corwin commented on the forthcoming celebration of the fifty-fourth anniversary of the settling of Marietta which was to take place on April 8, 1842. The newspaper was filled with letters of correspondence from Texas concerning Santa Anna and Sam Houston as well as local news (*Intelligencer* April 7, 1842).

The newspaper covered activities of the Washington Movement, a temperance society begun in Marietta in 1839. In April, 1842, the Washington Temperance Societies of the villages of Harmar and Marietta combined to hold a Temperance celebration. The meeting began with a Temperance Oration at 10:00 AM in the Methodist Church, followed by a business meeting at 2:00 PM. The Societies reassembled at the Congregational Church for a 6:30 PM meeting. Judge Warner of Athens, Ohio, was in attendance along with other distinguish visitors (*Intelligencer* April 7, 1842). The next great effort in temperance reform began in 1844. The central feature of this movement was total abstinence (Bennet 14).

The nation expanded the western frontier in 1843. John C. Fremont crossed the Rocky Mountains to California (Grun 408). Jefferson Davis, the future leader of the Confederacy, entered politics, and Charles Dickens published his work, *A Christmas Carol* (Grun 410). On April 6th the *Marietta Intelligencer* reported an earthquake was felt in Montpelier, Vermont, on the 14th of March. The paper reported murders in New York City, a stage robbery in Kentucky, and continued mutinies at sea. A reported mutiny on board the *U. S. John Adams* near the Cape of Good Hope was later contradicted with the arrival of the bark *Margarett Hugg* in the port of Norfolk. News from New Orleans announced the "emigration of one thousand people to the Oregon Territory." The wagon train will leave Fort Leavenworth, on the 1st of May (*Intelligencer* April 6 p2).

There was much excitement in Marietta during the month of November. Citizens awaited the Congregational Church bells to ring out, and village cannons to fire announcing the arrival of President John Quincy Adams, our sixth President (Williams 432). President Adams planned to visit Marietta, Ohio, on November 15, 1843 to tour the city. He had "consented" to lay the corner stone at the Cincinnati observatory and was traveling up river from Cincinnati on the boat *Ben Franklin*. The citizens of Marietta "tendered him an invitation" (Williams 433). When he arrived in the city he was shown the Ancient Mounds and Sacra Via Way (Bennet 12).

John Q. Adams was not the only prominent person to visit Marietta. King Phillipe, King of France, visited while in exile. He arrived in late January, 1798. The king had an excellent memory, and in later years remembered his visit to Marietta in great detail. As he explained, he left the boat to go into town to search for bread, and was referred to Mr. Thierry, a French baker. The baker had no bread on hand and instantly began heating his oven to supply the king's request. While the bread was baking, Phillipe amused himself by walking through the town, visiting the ancient mounds. He stopped here and there to sketch some of the earthworks. When Phillipe returned to the boat he found the ice on the Muskingum River had begun breaking apart. The baker had to leap onto the departing boat to deliver the freshly baked bread (Williams 431,432).

1844

James Knox Polk was elected the eleventh President. Elizabeth Barrett Browning published her work, *Poems* (Grun 410). During September the *Marietta Intelligencer* was filled with news from Washington City, New York, and New Orleans. The little village of Newport made the news. Mr. E. Adkins, a Newport resident, felt the comments he made at a Democratic meeting held in that village were misquoted by the editor. He was reported by the paper to say, when speaking of Great Britain, "he would rather that Texas should pass into her hands than to slavery." When pressed he retracted his statement and wrote the editor, insisting he said, "I would sooner trust [Texas] to the destiny of slavery, than suffer that our country pass into the power of Great Britain, etc." Of course the editor had the last word, and wrote, "many of Mr. Adkins' friends understood him and reported him as saying just what our correspondent understood and reported him to say" (*Intelligencer* Sept 5 p2). The issue of slavery was discussed throughout this nation. Marietta was a seagoing port. Two shipyards were located on the Muskingum river between Washington and Saca Via streets. The shipyards brought a good deal of money into the city. "Products of timber, rope and copper and the hands of skilled laborers" were needed. The ships were "built scientifically, and the honor of the Master Builder is placed into every plank, joint and bolt" (Bennet 5,6).

1846

The Mexican War began (Cram 262). News of the evacuation of Monterey, Mexico arrived in Marietta. An update on the First Ohio Regiment at the Battle of Monterey was received from John B. Weller, Lieut. Col 1st Reg OV (*Intelligencer* Nov 5, 1846).

The President's message coming from Washington City to Columbus, Ohio, on December 11, 1846, arrived with "unparalleled speed." The Ohio Stage Company picked the letter up on the western bank of the Ohio near Wheeling, West Virginia at 1:35 on Thursday, and delivered it to Columbus at 8:10 the same evening. A trip of "135 miles in six and one half hours" (Lee 351,352).

Marietta shipyards continued to flourish. In December, two vessels, soon to be delivered to a Lower Salem, Massachusetts firm, were lying in the Muskingum River. The barque *Marietta*, was completed January 31, 1847. She was one hundred feet long, twenty-four feet wide, and weighed 250 tons. She sailed downstream to Cincinnati, and was loaded with 2,000 barrels of pork and lard. The *Grace Darling* was launched in February, 1847. Another schooner in the process of construction was bound for New Orleans. The *New Orleans Times* reported, "two schooners and a barge built at Marietta, Ohio, are specimens of naval architecture that will vie with vessels of that class built in any of the eastern ship yards." In July 1847, the barque *John Farnum* sailed for Portsmouth. She was 104 feet long, 24 feet 3 inches wide, 275 tons, drafted six and one-half feet, and was fitted with ten staterooms. Once loaded with corn, she sailed for Cork, Ireland. A. B. Waters, who was in charge of the vessel, reported she arrived safely and the corn sold for $2.00 a bushel. In August 1847, the *John Farnum* docked at Philadelphia and the *Marietta* sailed from Boston to Cape Verde in twenty-six days. In April, 1848, the ship *Walhouding* (White Woman) "with its masts and ropes and well-made curves and lines" was completed. When launched she "swept from the bank into the Muskingum with the grace of a swan." A July, 1848 New York city newspaper praised the ship for her "beautiful lines, convenient construction, and sailing qualities" (Bennet 5,6). An excellent model of the John Farnum can be found at the Ohio River Museum in Marietta, Ohio.

1850

The United States population continued to grow rapidly. There were 23 million citizens; 3.2 million were black slaves (Grun 417).

The southern Governors of the States of Alabama, Tennessee, South Carolina, Georgia, and Virginia met. Their annual message "proclaims resistance to the last extremity any act of Congress to adopt a proviso or which abolishes slavery in the district of Columbia" (*Intelligencer* January 3). News from Washington City indicated "Mr. Calhoun's speech was read by Mr. Mason in the Senate on March 4th. He said, "Justice must be done to the South or the Union will be inevitably dissolved" (*Intelligencer* March 7 p2). On August 15th the paper reported, "Four male slaves belonging to Toomba and Stephens of Georgia last week attempted, at the instigation of whites, to escape from Washington. Police overtook the carriage containing the slaves from the city. The party in the carriage fired on the pursuers which was returned by the latter injuring two men badly" (*Intelligencer* August 15 p2). Henry Clay's *Compromise of Slavery Resolutions* was introduced to the United States Senate. It was accepted on September 9th. On September 12th, the Fugitive Slave Law passed (Cram 262).

Earlier in the year, the thirteenth President, Millard Fillmore, settled a conflict, not one of government. A dispatch from Washington dated February 28th indicated, "The difficulty between Messrs. Bissell and Davis was settled the evening previous, by the personal intervention of the President. They were to have fought this morning with muskets at a distance of fifteen paces" (*Intelligencer* March 7 p2). There was much speculation as to whom might be the author of *Jane Eyre*. The paper updated the public, and reported the author was "now said to be a Miss Bronte, a lady of Bradford, in Yorkshire" (*Intelligencer* Jan 31). Two American authors made their mark; Nathaniel Hawthorne published *The Scarlet Letter* and Emerson published *The Representative Men* (Grun 416).

California was granted statehood (Grun 416). Some Harmer and Marietta men left the area to work the gold fields of California. "A dozen letters were received from Marietta and Harmar men, all of whom were well, and, so far as we have heard doing well" (*Intelligencer* August 15 p2). News from California indicated large gold shipments sailed to the port of New Orleans. Between April 11th and June 1st "$13,000,000 to $14,000,000 in gold dust" left San Francisco for New Orleans (Intelligencer August 15 p2).

"The manufacturing of boats and shoes employed more people than any other single business in Marietta" (*Intelligencer* Jan 3). The paper prioritized boat and river news. The 1849 statistics on steamboat disasters made the front page. The names of all boats sunk, burned, and otherwise destroyed on the western waters were alphabetically listed. The 83 destroyed boats had a dollar value of $1,600,400. Very few of these boats could be raised or repaired (*Intelligencer* February 7, 1).

The population of Harmar in 1850 was 1,006 (Howe 607). Harmar will be annexed into the city of Marietta by vote, on April 1, 1890 (Austin 76). The population of Marietta in 1850 was 3,133 (Howe 607).

1851

Cold February had not smothered the fires of temperance. "The Sons of Temperance of Marietta and Harmar turned out in procession on Friday evening last, and made a fine display. Nearly 300 were in procession...about 500 persons have signed the temperance pledge and in the last two weeks 70-80 men have been received into the "Order of the Sons" (*Intelligencer* February 6 p2).

France continued to be of interest to the citizens of Washington County. The support France gave this country during the revolution was not forgotten. The local newspaper reported on the citizens of France and revealed their current activities. Attention was given to the smallest detail including the significance of dress "...So long as the people of France dress like gentlemen, so long the government feels perfectly safe from insurrections and outbreaks, but the very moment the citizens take to wearing their shirts outside of their pantaloons that very moment the cabinet is seized with consternation, and as if the bricks had already commenced flying" (*Intelligencer* February 27 p2).

Any news concerning the Lafayette family remained worthy of reporting in America, particularly the good fortune of the Marques George Washington Lafayette. The Lafayette family received 2,400,000 francs, $480,000, from a lawsuit. Madame du Cayla, the most "prominent female in the Court of Restoration" entered into the suit on behalf of the Marquis for half of the proceeds after he refused to proceed on his own. She won the suit by utilizing some important papers that fell into her hands upon the death of Marques de Lasignan. Mme du Cayla was an extremely political woman. In her youth she was considered to be much more than a friend to Louis

XVII for she was described as being "young, beautiful, accomplished, and endowed with great talents." The Charter of 1814 was signed in her chateau, Saint Queu (*Intelligencer* October 29).

General Marie Joseph Paul Yves Roch Gilbert du Motier Marquess de la Lafayette and his son George Washington Lafayette visited Marietta, Ohio, in 1825. They were returning from a tour of the southwest aboard the steamboat *Mechanic*. The Marietta boat, under Captain Wyllys Hall, left Nashville, Tennessee on the sixth of May. On May 8th, in the night, one hundred and twenty-five miles below Louisville, Kentucky, the *Mechanic* hit a snag which pierced the boat upward through the main deck. Captain Hall examined the boat and realized it was "useless" to make any effort to save it. He gathered Lafayette, his son George W., a Mr. La Vasener and a twelve-year-old girl who belonged to a passenger into a boat, and skulled the boat to a nearby shore with all possible speed. Captain Hall continued to transport passengers to shore until he was overcome with exhaustion. He gave the boat to Governor Carroll of Tennessee. The Governor, a skilled boatman, saved the remaining passengers. John Hunt, the *Mechanic's* clerk, tried to save the steamer's money and books, but the boat careened; he and the desk fell into the water. "All this transpired in less than twenty-five minutes." Lafayette was eventually rescued and returned to Louisville, Kentucky. He continued his journey on the Ohio aboard the steamboat *Herald*, and arrived in Marietta on Monday morning, May 23rd. Lafayette left the boat for a reception at the mansion of Nahum Ward, Esq., whom he had previously met in Paris. His arrival was announced to the citizens of Marietta by the sound of a cannon, and people began to "flock" around him "to seize his hand and welcome him to the soil he so nobly defended" (Williams 432). The *Mechanic* was built by John Mitchell on the Little Muskingum River in Washington County, Ohio. It was fitted in "good style after the manner of the eastern boats." She had a 96 foot keel and was 18 foot wide. Phillip and Wise of Steubenville built the engine for ample power and good speed. She was "equal to any boat on the western waters" (Letter from Wyllys Hall to Dr. S.P. Hildreth April 25, 1859).

American authors published great works this year. Hawthorn wrote *The House of Seven Gables*; Longfellow, published *The Golden Legend*; Herman Melville penned *Moby Dick* (Grun 416).

The year 1851 ended in disaster. On or about December 25th a fire ravaged the capital. Thirty-five thousand volumes of books were destroyed along with Stuart's paintings of the first five Presidents, an original portrait of Columbus, a portrait of Bolivar, a statue of Jefferson, Apollo by Mills, and a bust of Lafayette by David (*Intelligencer* December 31 p2).

1852

Franklin Pierce was elected the fourteenth President. Two new books provided excellent reading and helped Mary pass the long dull winter nights in Malta, Ohio. Charles Dickens published *Bleak House* and Harriet Beecher Stowe of Cincinnati published *Uncle Tom's Cabin* (Grun 418). Stowe hoped to buy a new silk dress with the profits she earned from the sale of this book (O'Bryant 213). The novel became the first American best seller, and was later translated into twenty languages (O'Bryant 215).

1857 - 1858

These were the years of floods and rain, of iced over rivers, and heightened passions. James Buchanan was the new President of the United States (Grun 420).

In February 1857, ice froze "firm" on the Mississippi River, and reached a depth of thirty-five inches on the Allegheny River at Pittsburgh. Rain fell in "torrents" on the gold miners in California (*Intelligencer* February 18, 1857). The flow of gold from California was now directed to New York City. Docking steamers held millions in gold dust.

The tempers of the elected representatives in Washington reached a breaking point in March. Wright of Tennessee and Harris of

Maryland fought on the floor of Congress. "A duel is rumored." Mr. David Hume of Virginia was shot in the Pension office by Mr. D. C. Lee (Intelligencer March 4, 1857). President Buchanan was fully aware of the deep divisions within the government and the country. In his inaugural address, he appealed to the virtues of common sense and reason. He also raised the question of a free or slave state by the "principle of popular sovereignty," and stated that under the constitution "slavery in the States is beyond reach of any human power, except that of the respective States themselves wherein it exists...whilst it has been productive of no positive good to any human being, it has been the prolific source of great evils to the master, to the slave, and to the whole country. It has alienated and estranged the people of the sister States from each other, and has even seriously endangered the very existence of the Union..."

Buchanan also proposed that the expanding country was bound together by free trade through railroads, rivers, canals, and seas, and questioned the intelligence of "arresting its free progress by the geographical lines of jealous and hostile States." He was most embarrassed about the financial condition of our nation. The treasury had too large a surplus of monies. He intended to use this surplus to enlarge the navy so greater protection could be offered California and the shipping lanes around the Isthmus of Central America (*Intelligencer* March 11, 1857).

His address to the nation went unheeded. Battle lines were drawn in the Kansas Territory. The newspaper reported Pro-Slavery men committed acts of "lynchings, shootings, scalping, arson, fraud, and plunder." The paper also reported that it was the "Free State emigrants" who made all the trouble, and the Pro-Slavery "folks" were as "peaceable and well disposed as need be." Gov. Shannon, the most pliant of Ohio Pro-Slavery men, admitted that they compelled his participation in outrages that even he revolted at and finally hustled him home with threats and violence. The third governor of Kansas, Mr. Geary, "just returned from the Territory, and glad to escape with his life, [related] how they plotted his assassination."

A Pennsylvania man, Robert J. Walker, accepted the appointment as Governor of Kansas (*Intelligencer* April 8, 1857). News from St. Louis indicated the battle for Kansas continued. Walker camped outside Lawrence with eight companies of dragoons on July 17th. The citizens of Lawrence chose not to negotiate with him, and decided not resist the troops unless they were fired upon when civil war was declared. Walker carried warrants for the arrest of city officers and other citizens of Lawrence (*Intelligencer* July 29, 1857). The October 21st paper reported that balloting was over; Kansas was declared a Free State. This election was a bitter pill; one not easily swallowed by the Pro-Slavery movement. The State of Mississippi was actively importing slaves directly from Africa (*Intelligencer* October 21, 1857).

The Lincoln and Douglas debates began in 1858.

Quite by accident, while searching for salt, oil was discovered in Noble County in 1814 near the village of Olive, now known as Caldwell. James Dutton drilled the first producing oil well in 1860, and sold the daily production of 118 barrels for $20 a barrel. The Macksburg land formation held five to six stratum of oil-bearing sand. Over time the field expanded to twelve to fifteen miles squared (Austin 228). The first light crude oil sold in the city of Marietta was purchased in the summer of 1860. Ninety barrels were sent to Zanesville for refining. The first Marietta oil refinery was constructed outside the corporation limits in 1861 (Austin 59-61).

1861   The War Of The Rebellion

"The people of the States formed out of the Northwest Territory [Ohio, Illinois, Indiana, Michigan and Wisconsin] were by education and tradition, and more especially by virtue of the molding power of a great fundamental law, opposed to slavery and to the doctrine of States Rights. They naturally went with the North: and we believe we are justified in saying that the North could not have succeeded in the war for the Union if the States formed from the Northwest Territory had refused to co-operate" (Austin 32). "On the evening of January 8, 1861, pursuant to a call for a Union meeting, the people of Marietta and vicinity" assembled at the court house. There they condemned the secession movement and affirmed "their devotion to the cause of the Union" (Austin 32).

Other states voted for secession. Mississippi seceded January 9th; Florida, Alabama, Georgia, and Louisiana followed on January 10th and February 1st; Virginia seceded April 17th, Arkansas, May 6th, Tennessee, May 9th, and North Carolina, May 20th (Cram 286).

The Confederate Government was organized at Montgomery, Alabama, on February 8th. Jefferson Davis was elected President, and Alexander H. Stephens, Vice President on February 9th. Abraham Lincoln was inaugurated the sixteenth President of the Union on March 4th. A year earlier in 1860, President-elect Abraham Lincoln declined "a request to furnish liquors to the national committee sent to inform him of his nomination to the Presidency"; he returned unopened the hampers of wines and liquors sent to him (Cherrington 153,154).

Beauregard bombarded Fort Sumter, South Carolina, on April 12th (Cram 264). The Civil War began. News of the bombardment reached Marietta on Saturday morning, April 13th, and on Monday morning the news of President Lincoln's call for seventy-five thousand men arrived in Marietta (Austin 33). The Battle of Big Bethel, Virginia, was fought on June 10th. McDowell was defeated at the Battle of Bull Run, Virginia, on July 21st (Cram 264). "The disaster of Bull Run was credited largely to account of drunkenness" (Cherrington 155). President Lincoln signed an act of Congress forbidding the sale or conveyance of intoxicating drinks to soldiers (Cherrington 154).

Quoting *The New York Tribune*, the *Intelligencer* reported the November 1st Union troop strength stood at 400,000 men. Ohio boldly volunteered 51,000 men. Only the States of New York and Pennsylvania volunteered more: New York, 78,000; Pennsylvania, 54,000 (*Intelligencer* October 30 p 1).

Classified ads directed toward the "brave" volunteers filled the *Marietta Intelligencer* (November 20, 1861). Mr. C. E. Glines advertised Blunts' War Maps of Virginia, Delaware, Maryland, and other military goods, "Just Received." Mr. Barker advertised boots:

Infantry Volunteers
It is a saving of Money and Health to wear Boots
Are the best for a Winter Campaign
Come & Buy # 19 Front St. G. W. Barker

1862

The iron ships, the *Merrimack* and the *Monitor*, battled in the James River at Hampton Roads, Virginia, on March 9th (Cram 286). Grant defeated Beauregard in the Battle of Pittsburgh Landing (Shiloh, Tennessee); 20,000 Union men were lost April 6th and 7th. New Orleans, Louisiana was captured by Farragut's fleet on April 25th (Cram 264). McClellan won a victory at the Battle of Seven Pines and Fair Oaks, Virginia on May 31st and June 1st. On June 3rd, Lee was appointed Chief of Command of the Confederate Army. Lee and McClellan clashed at the Seven Day's Battles in Virginia, June 26th to July 1st. From August 26th to September 1st Pope's battles between Manassas and Washington raged. Lee invaded Maryland, crossing the Potomac River near Point of Rocks on September 4th through the 7th (Cram 264). McClellan and Lee engaged at the Battle of Anteitan, Maryland, September 17th. On December 13th, Lee won the Battle of Fredericksburg, Virginia. Twelve thousand Federals died (Cram 264).

1863

The war raged on. President Lincoln issued the *Emancipation Proclamation* on January 1st (Cram 264). Thus "striking the shackles from three million slaves" (Austin 37).

The Federals bombarded Fort Sumter, South Carolina, on April 7th. Lee was victorious at the Battle of Chancellorsville, Virginia, on

May 2-3; 18,000 Union men fell. Early fought on May 3-4 in the Battle of Fredericksburg, and won. Lee invaded Maryland and Pennsylvania in June. On July 1-3, Meade and Lee engaged in the Battle of Gettysburg, Pennsylvania and 50,000 men were lost (Cram 264). On July 4th, Vicksburg, Virginia fell and the Union rejoiced (Austin 37).

1864

General Sherman's raid from Vicksburg, Virginia reached Meridian, Mississippi on February 14th (Cram 264). The Union reelected Abraham Lincoln to a second term. General Ulysses S. Grant succeeded General Halleck as Commander-in-Chief of the Union Armies. Grant visited Washington for three days. He conferred privately with Stanton and Halleck. He dined with Secretary of State William H. Seward and visited Meade. He spent limited time with Lincoln, and much of it was in the presence of the cabinet. Grant recalled that in his first private meeting with Lincoln, Lincoln said, "he had never professed to be a military man or to know how campaigns should be conducted, and never wanted to interfere in them: but that procrastination on the part of commanders, and the pressure from the people at the North and Congress, which was always with him, forced him into issuing his series of military orders, some of which he conceded were mistaken. Lincoln added that "while armies were sitting down waiting for opportunities to turn up which might, perhaps, be more favorable from a strictly military point of view, the government was spending millions of dollars every day; that there was a limit to the sinews of war, and a time might be reached when the spirits and resources of the people would become exhausted." He simply wanted someone to "take the responsibility and act," something Grant assured him that he would do. Lincoln said he did not want to know what Grant proposed to do but brought out a plan of his own to use the Potomac as a base and advance between two streams that would protect the Union flanks. Grant realized, but did not mention to Lincoln, that these streams would also shield Lee. Thereafter, said Grant, he did not communicate his plans to Lincoln, Stanton, or Halleck" (Boritt 166,167).

A torn and bloody Union turned to God; the federal mint printed "In God We Trust" on United States coinage (Grun 427).

Mary wrote of a vacant chair and an empty fireside. Both North and South embraced the song, *The Vacant Chair*, which was written in November, 1861. Words are by H. S. Washburn. George F. Root wrote the music. This song commemorates the death of Lt. John William Gout of Massachusetts who was killed at Ball's Bluff, October, 1861 (Glass 286,287).

A Federal newsman, Charles Carleton Coffin, of the *Boston Journal* reported the following song was sung by Union troops at the Battle of Antietam after "the sun went down, the thunder died away, and the musketry ceased. Bivouac fires gleamed out as if a great city had lighted its lamps" (Wheeler 194).

> "Do they miss me at home? Do they miss me?
> Twould be an assurance most dear
> To know that this moment some loved one
> Were saying, "I wish he were here,"
> To feel that the group at the fireside were
> thinking of me as I roam;
> Oh, yes, 'twould be joy beyond measure
> To know that they miss me at home."

The war continued. Grant and Lee fought the Battles of the Wilderness on May 5th through the 7th, 30,000 men were lost. On May 7th, Sherman began his Georgia Campaign. He marched from Chattanooga, Tennessee, with 110,000 men (Cram 264). To quote Sherman, "You cannot qualify war in harsher terms than I will. War is cruelty and you can not refine it" (Boritt 154).

The Battle of Cold Harbor, Virginia, was fought June 1st-3rd. General Grant fought the Battle of Petersburg June 16th-18th; he was repulsed and 10,000 men died. On June 18th Grant began the siege of Petersburg, Virginia (Cram 264).

To break the Petersburg siege, coal miners of the 48th Pennsylvania dug a tunnel beneath Confederate lines. They filled the end with explosives, and detonated a devastating blast. The Union troops failed to exploit the opening; they were repulsed and suffered heavy losses. Grant called this battle the "saddest affair I have witnessed in this war." The day after the Battle of the Crater, Lincoln arrived at Fort Monroe. He conferred with Grant for five hours. So little was known of their discussion that the noted historian T. Harry Williams wondered if they had actually met; yet they did meet (Boritt 178).

The ship *Alabama* was sunk off Cherbourg, France, on June 19th. Sherman fought The Battle of Kenesaw Mountain, Georgia, on the 27th, and was repulsed (Cram 264). In the Fall and Winter, Sherman moved South. He occupied Atlanta on September 2nd and Savannah on December 22nd. When Savannah fell on December 22, 1864, Sherman wrote Lincoln, "I beg to present you a Christmas gift, the city of Savannah, with 150 heavy guns and plenty of ammunition, and also about 25,000 bales of cotton." Lincoln replied, "When you were about leaving Atlanta for the Atlantic Coast, I was anxious if not fearful, but feeling that you were the better judge and remembering that 'nothing risked, nothing gained,' I did not interfere. Now, the undertaking being a success, the honor is all yours; for I believe none of us went further than to acquiesce" (Boritt 156).

1865

General Grant occupied Petersburg and Richmond, Virginia on April 3rd. Lee surrendered to Grant at Appomattox Court House, Virginia, April 9, 1865 (Cram 264). Ohio's Governor Brough issued a proclamation announcing the victory and recommended April 14th, the anniversary of the fall of Fort Sumter, as a "fitting day to celebrate the fall of the Rebellion" (Austin 38).

President Lincoln was assassinated at Washington D.C., April 14th (Cram 264). Vice President Johnson succeeded Lincoln on April 15th (Cram 286).

At the close of the war, 200,000 Union soldiers assembled for review in Washington D.C. "No liquor [was] allowed to be sold in the national capital and drunkenness [was] entirely absent from the celebration" (Cherrington 158).

Union troops were freed from Confederate prison camps at Andersonville and Cahaba in April. These survivors and civilians were "jammed" aboard the steamboat *Sultana* at Vicksburg, Mississippi. Over two thousand four hundred passengers crowded onto a boat designed to hold three hundred and seventy-six. The *Sultana* steamed north against the current. On April 27, 1865, during the night just north of Memphis, Tennessee, the boiler on this Cincinnati-built steamboat exploded. Flames engulfed the overloaded boat. The flooded Mississippi River was three miles wide. The current was fast, and the water high. Wounded, diseased, malnutritioned Union soldiers were drowned; approximately 1,800 died. Only a few hundred survivors were pulled from the water. The Federal Government performed a limited investigation concerning the overloaded boat and allegations of bribery. A marine disaster exceeding that of the *Titanic* was swept under the Federal carpet (Potter).

Jefferson Davis was captured on May 10th and imprisoned at Fortress Monroe from 1865 until 1867. Slavery was abolished on December 18, 1865 (Cram 286). Ohio sent 304,814 white volunteers and 5,092 black volunteers to fight for the Union cause; 35,475 Ohio volunteers lost their lives in this conflict.

1866 – 1867

The United States Congress passed the Civil Rights Bill on April 12, 1866 (Cram 286). "In its darkest hours, following the Civil War, the nearly moribund temperance movement began to stir with fresh life" (Kobler 95).

On March 2, 1867 the Reconstruction Act passed over a President's veto. (Cram 266). The National Temperance Convention was held in Cleveland, Ohio. (Cherrington 162).

R. O. Clark, the subject of one of Mary's poems, was mentioned in an article in the *Marietta Times*, April 1, 1886. "Robert Clark, who several years ago moved from this vicinity of South Olive [Noble Co.] to Michigan was some time ago killed in that State, by a railroad train. He was employed in a lumber camp. One of the men was taken sick, and it was necessary to send him to the hospital. Clark went on the railroad track and flagged the fast train but before he could get out of the way, it struck and threw him into a snowdrift. Death was instantaneous."

Roderick D. Gambrell, age twenty-one, editor of the temperance paper *Sword and Shield,* was murdered in May by Colonel Jones S. Hamilton and other assailants in Jackson, Mississippi. Colonel Hamilton secured a change of venue to Rankin County, Mississippi, and was acquitted after a lengthy trial. Roderick's father was Dr. J. H. Gambrell, a nationally noted editor and lecturer (Mississippi Archives, documents 5/31/94).

1870 – 1871

On October 10-12 Chicago burned. Damages were estimated to be $300,000,000 (Cram 266).

From the 1870's through the 1880's the Temperance Movement gained strength. The "Crusade of 1873 and the organization of the Women's Christian Temperance Union in 1874 marked the entrance into the active movement for temperance reform of the women of America." The Women's Crusade had its start in Hillsboro, Ohio, on December 24, 1873 (Cherington 169,170). "At the height of the Crusade 17,000 small-town Ohio saloons, drugstores, and other dispensers of drink by glass temporarily went out of business, and 1,000 followed in New York state. All together, throughout the country, almost 30,000 closed. Eight of Ohio's biggest distilleries and 750 breweries" elsewhere suspended operations. As a result of these closings beer consumption declined by 6,000,000 gallons.

1880

The village of Macksburg is located 25 miles North of Marietta, Ohio, in Aurelius Township, Washington County. In 1880, the 149 residents of this small village moved both passengers and freight on the Cincinnati and Marietta Railroad (Cram 291). Although Macksburg was situated in the center of the Ohio coal fields, petroleum was the single most important product.

When Ohio Republican James A. Garfield ran for the presidency in 1880, women were led to believe he was a "true friend of the temperance cause" (Cherrington 171).

1881

Emigration to America continued. In the first nine months of 1881, five hundred and sixty thousand new citizens arrived (Cram 266). The tenth national census of 1880 indicated the country's population had risen to fifty million (Cram 266).

The twentieth President, James Abram Garfield, born on November 19, 1831 in a log cabin in Orange, Cuyahoga County, Ohio, walked to Cleveland at the age of sixteen. He was determined to find employment on a lake schooner, but instead accepted an offer from his cousin, Amos Letcher, to work as a canal boatman between the coal mines at Brierhill and Cleveland. When Garfield ran for election in Ohio in 1857 and 1858 he was known as an effective speaker, and an ardent antislavery man. He was elected to the Ohio Senate in 1859. When the call came for 75,000 troops during the war of the Rebellion, he moved that Ohio furnish 20,000 soldiers and three million dollars as her share for the Union cause. Garfield volunteered for the war, and took part in the Battle of Shiloh on the second day. He fought at Chickamauga, and was made a Major-General of the volunteers for gallantry in battle. He was inaugurated President on March 4, 1881.

Garfield was shot by Charles J. Guiteau on July 2, 1881 at a Washington railway station while on his way to attend commencement exercises at his alma mater, Williams College. He died from blood poisoning in Long Branch, New Jersey on September 19, 1881. On that same day Chester A. Arthur was inaugurated President in New York City (Encyclopedia Britannica 464,465). The English, Belgian and Spanish courts went into mourning for eight days. A wreath of white rosebuds sent by Queen Victoria was placed at the foot of his coffin (Barnhart 242). On January 25th, the assassin, Guiteau, was found guilty of murder. He was hanged on June 30, 1882 (Cram 266).

1884

Serious floods moved through the Ohio Valley (Cram 286).

Mary wrote poetry in Noble County at Crooked Tree, population 75, and Dexter City, population 150. She also wrote while in Washington County at Macksburg and Sand Hill. Sand Hill was more area than village. It was not listed in the 1888 Cram's Atlas under towns. Cram listed all towns and cities with a population of ten or more (Cram 305).

Ulysses Simpson Grant, General and eighteenth President, died at Mount M'Gregor, New Jersey, on July 23, 1885. In 1884, the *Century Magazine* approached Grant with a request for some articles. He undertook the work to keep the "wolf from the door." The offer was a blessing and the writing proved to be a "congenial task." Grant found writing to be so appealing that he compiled his personal memoirs into a "frank, modest and charming" book which ranks as one of the best standard military biographies ever published. Through the sale of these publications Grant earned approximately $500,000. The circumstances under which he accomplished this task was "an act of heroism comparable with any Grant ever showed as a soldier." During most of this time he suffered the "tortures" of throat cancer. Grant finished the manuscript four days before his death. (Encyclopedia Britannica vol. XII 358). Born at Point Pleasant, Ohio, on

April 27, 1822, Grant was the first man to run against a woman for the Presidency. He ran against Victoria Claflin Woodhull, a Homer, Ohio, suffragette pioneer and Free Love advocate (O'Bryant 33,134).

1885-1886

Stephen Grover Cleveland was nominated for President three times on the Democratic ticket and elected twice. He served from 1885 to 1889, and 1893 to 1897. His father, a clergyman in the Presbyterian Church, was a descendant of Moses Cleveland who emigrated from Ipswich, England to Massachusetts in 1635. Grover was considered to be one of the leaders of the western New York bar. In 1884, he ran for President against a disorganized Republican party on a platform for "radical reforms" and won. He desired to reorganize government in the areas of civil service, national finance, and administration. In his first term, Cleveland vetoed 413 bills passed by Congress. During this term he married Miss Frances Folsom, the daughter of his law partner. During the second term, he succeeded in repealing the silver legislation. When this very independent man retired from office, he became a trustee of Princeton University and a Stafford Little lecturer. He published two books: *Presidential Problems* in 1904, and *Fishing and Hunting Sketches* in 1906 (Encyclopedia Britannica 501-503).

The nation was rapidly expanding both geographically and industrially; 128,407 miles of railroad track wound its way through the land. Additional track was being laid at a rate of 3,028 miles per year (Cram 290).

Bartholdi's Statue of Liberty arrived in New York City on June 19, 1885 (Cram 266).

In 1885 and 1886 in Noble County, Ohio, oil wells were drilled and coal was mined. Horses were bred and sold to eastern carriage owners. Thoroughbred Kentucky race horses continued to be a sport for the wealthy. The Caldwell Fair Company let a contract out for a Grand Stand that seated one thousand people (*Marietta Times* Sept 17

1885). Tobacco was the farmer's money crop. The paper reported, "the tobacco crop has been saved in excellent condition" (*Marietta Times* Oct 22, 1885). During March, 1886 the Caldwell Woolen Mill increased its capacity for room and work, and another knitting factory was opened. Surplus power from the flour mill was to run it. Also in March, a group of over 125 people left Caldwell for Kansas (*Marietta Times* March 18, 1886).

Fife Lake, Michigan is located in Grand Traverse County. Fife Lake had a population of 350 in the 1880's. Many Ohioans moved into this area of Michigan.

Other Notes:

Howe's Grove sits on land originally owned by Revolutionary War General Rufus Putnam. The General gave his daughter and her husband Perley Howe the farm in 1798. His grandson, George A. Howe, lived in the family home next to the grove. George's daughter, Miss Persis, the last remaining Howe, gave the grove to the State of Ohio, on January 17, 1950 (Lee 1). The name Belpre was derived from the contracted French noun, "Belleprairie," meaning "beautiful meadow" (Dickinson 5).

The 62nd Ohio Infantry fought at the battles of Port Republic, Virginia, June 9, 1862, Blackwater, Virginia, December 12, 1862, Fort Wagner, South Carolina, July to September 6, 1963, the second assault on Fort Wagner on July 18, 1863 and the evacuation of the Fort on September 7, 1863 (Official Roster of the Solders of the State of Ohio). They also participated in the battle of Deep Bottom Run, Virginia from August 14-18 (Boatner 230,231).

GLOSSARY

acrostic (a-kros tik) n. a composition, usually in verse, in which a given set of letters taken in order, as the first letter of each line, form a motto, phrase, name, or word (Lewis 8)

allay (a-la) v.t. to abate or lessen; syn. moderate, reduce, relieve, to quiet or calm (Lewis 18)

alloy (a-loi) n. an admixture of good with evil (Lewis 19)

anon (a-non) adv. soon; in a little while; at another time; again (Lewis 26)

athwart (a-thwort) adv. across; from side to side; crosswise (Lewis 41)

bark n. a small three-masted vessel with foremast and mainmast, squared-rigged and mizzenmast fore-and-aft rigged. Poetic, small ship; also barque (Lewis 55)

betide (be tid) v.t. to happen to; befall, as woe betide the wander (Lewis 66)

boon (boon) adj. jovial, merry, archaic or poetic, kind; bounteous (Lewis 78)

bourne (born; boorm) n. a boundary limit; a place aimed at; a goal (Lewis 80)

bud n. a young girl in her first season in society, to be like a young flower in youth and freshness (Lewis 90).

debauchee (deb o she) n. a dissipated person; drunkard (Lewis 181)

delve (delv) v.t. archaic to dig (Lewis 188)

dissemble (di sem bl) v.t. to hide under a false appearance as to act the hypocrite (Lewis 207)

dram-shops n. a barroom; a place where liquor is sold (Lewis 216)

Elysian (Ely sian) used by Milton (river of bliss), Carlyle (brightness), Byron (when heart meets heart again in dreams) taken from Elysium – "the abode of the blessed" dead, used in Greek mythology (Simpson 152)

emending (e-mend ing) to alter or correct, as a text (Lewis 231)

ensanguine (en-sang gwin) v.t. to smear or cover with blood (Lewis 236)

ether (e ther) n. the upper, purer air; which, when inhaled, produces unconsciousness and insensibility to pain (Lewis 242)

fain (fan) adv. willingly; gladly; as I would fain to do your pleasure; adj. glad, willing, constrained (Lewis 252)

feign (fan) v.t. and v.i. pretend, simulate, as to feign illness (Lewis 258)

fratricide (frat ri-cid or fra fri-sid) n. the crime of killing a brother or sister (Lewis 280,816)

genial (je ni-al) adj. kindly and sympathetic; cordial (Lewis 294)

Golconda (gol-kon'da) n. ruined city, India; noted for diamond cutting (Lewis 874); the old name of Hyderabad formerly celebrated for its diamonds, used as a synonym to a "mine of wealth" (Simpson 652)

Haman (hei man) n. the name of the chief minister of Ahasuerus who was hanged on the gallows prepared for Mordecai, as related in the Book of Esther, used allusively (phr. to hang as high as Haman) (Simpson 1054)

hie (hi) v.t. to cause to hasten; to urge; incite; v.i. to hasten; hurry as; hie thee hence (Lewis 330)

hillock (hil uk) n. a small hill or elevation; mounds (Lewis 331)

jar p.p. to give out with a harsh sound; be discordant (Lewis 384)

knell (nel) n. the sound of a bell when struck, esp. a funeral bell; hence, a sign of coming evil; v.i. to toll dolefully (Lewis 395)

lee (le) n. the direction opposite to that from which the wind blows; the side which is protected from the wind; shelter (Lewis 406)

Mon Chere Aime (mon shar a mi) Fr. my dear friend (Lewis 851)

myriads (mir i ad) n. ten thousand; hence a very large number; as the sky at night is covered with myriads of stars (Lewis 466)

pall (pall) n. a covering for a coffin, hearse or tomb (Lewis 503)

pinions (pin yuns) adj. in reference to things poetically represented as having wings 1732 Pope, Ess. Man; 1791 E. Darwin, Bot. Garden; 1850 Neale Hymn, "The Strain Upraise of Joy and Praise", Ye winds on pinions light! (Simpson and Weiner 867,868)

prate (prat) v.i. to prattle; talk idly; v.t. to utter without sense or meaning (Lewis 549)

proferred (prof er) v.t. to offer for acceptance; as to proffer assistance (Lewis 559)

repining (ri-pin'ing) v.i. p.p. to fret oneself; complain; feel discontent (Lewis 600)

resplendent (re splen dent) adj. shining brilliantly; intensely bright; splendid (Lewis 604)

retinue (ret i nu) n. the body of persons who attend a prince or person of distinction; a train of attendants (Lewis 606)

rift (rift) n. an opening made by splitting; cleft; as, a rift in a cloud (Lewis 611)

ruminate (ru min ate) v.i. to mediate, or muse; reflect (Lewis 622)

sable (sa bl) n. mourning dress, dark colored; black (Lewis 624)

schooner (skoon er) n. a vessel with two or more masts, rigged fore and aft (Lewis 635)

Sirius (Sir i us) n. the Dog Star, the most brilliant star in the sky (Lewis 667)

sloop n. a one-masted vessel with a fore-and-aft rig (Lewis 672)

somber (som ber) adj. dull, dark (Lewis 681)

tares (tar) n. any of a genus of herbs of the pea family, mostly climbing; in the Bible, an unidentified weed generally understood to be darnel; Matthew, Chapter 13:25,36 (Lewis 732)

tracery (tras er i) n. a fine, delicately executed design (Lewis 758)

verdant (vur dant) adj. covered with fresh green grass or foliage; having the freshness of spring (Lewis 797)

waft (waft) v.i. and v.t. to float, or cause to float, along through the air or on water (Lewis 807)

ween (wen) v.i. archaic, to suppose; think; as I ween (Lewis 815)

wert (wurt) archaic or poetic, second person singular, past indicative and subjunctive, of the verb be (Lewis 816)

BIBLIOGRAPHY

Andrews, Martin R. *History of Marietta and Washington County, Ohio and Representative Citizens.* Chicago, IL: Biographical Publishing Co., 1902.

Austin, L. G. Compiler. *Historical and Business Review: Washington County, Ohio For The Year 1891.* Coshocton, OH: Union Publishing Company, 1891.

Bailey, Elmer. *Religious Thought In The Greater American Poets.* Boston, MA and Chicago, IL: The Pilgrim Press, 1922.

Barnhart, Clarence L. ed. *New Century Cyclopedia of Names.* New York, NY: Appleton Century Crofts, Inc., 1954.

Bennet, W. P. *Marietta in The Forties And Her Evolution In Human Affairs.* Marietta, OH: no date.

Boatner, Mark Mayo. *The Civil War Dictionary.* New York, NY: David McKay Company Inc., 1959.

Boritt, Gabor S., ed. *Lincoln's Generals.* New York, NY: Oxford University Press, 1994.

Cherrington, Ernest H. *The Evolution of Prohibition in the United States of America.* Westerville, OH: The American Issue Press, 1920.

Cist, Charles. *Cincinnati in 1841: Its Early Annuals and Future Prospects.* Cincinnati, OH: Printed and published by the author, 1841.

Cist, Charles. *Cincinnati in 1851: Sketches and Statistics.* Cincinnati, OH: Wm. H. Moore and Co., 1851.

Cram, George F. *Cram's Universal Atlas 1888: Geographical, Astronomical and Historical.* First edition. Cincinnati, OH: M.A. Harris & Co., cc. 1887.

Dickens, Charles. *American Notes.* New York, NY: Harper and Brothers, 1842.

Dickinson, Cornelius Evarts, D.D. *A History of Belpre: Washington County, Ohio.* Parkersburg, WV: Globe Printing & Binding Company, 1920.

Encyclopedia Britannica, vol XI, XII. 11th ed. Cambridge, England: The University Press, 1910.

Eynon, Nola R. *Noble County Cemeteries.* Caldwell Public Library, Caldwell, OH. 1965.

Franklin County Ohio Marriage Records. CD Rom. Marietta Public Library, Marietta, OH: 1846.

Gates, Beman and Andrews, T. L., eds. *The Marietta Intelligencer.* Microfilm. Marietta College, Marietta, OH. 1842 -1861.

Glass, Paul. *Singing Soldiers: A History of the Civil War in Song.* New York, NY: Grosset & Dunlap, 1968.

Grun, Bernard. *The Timetables of History: A Horizontal Linkage of People and Events.* New Updated Edition. New York, NY: Simon & Schuster, Inc., 1979.

Harris, Laurie Lanzen. *Nineteenth Century Edition Literature Criticism.* Detroit, MI: Gale Research Company, 1981.

Hildreth, S. P., MD. *Hildreth Letters.* Dawes Memorial Library, Marietta College, Marietta, OH: no date.

History of Noble County. *Portraits and Biographical Sketches of some of its Pioneers and Prominent Men.* Chicago, IL: L. H. Watkins and Co., no date.

Howe, Henry. *Historical Collections of Ohio: General and Local History.* Cincinnati, OH: Published by author at E. Morgan & Co., 1852.

Kobler, John. *Ardent Spirits, The Rise and Fall of Prohibition.* New York, NY: G. P. Putnam's Sons, 1973.

Lee, Alfred E. (AM) *History of the City of Columbus Ohio Capital of Ohio.* vol 1. New York, NY and Chicago, IL: Munsell & Company, 1892.

Lee, Ruth A. *Howe's Grove.* A personal letter. 1994.

Lewis, William D., and Brown, Thomas Kite, Jr., eds. *The Secretary's Desk Book*: including the *Winston Simplified Dictionary.* Philadelphia, PA: International Press, John C. Winston Company Proprietors, 1932.

Lytton, Edward Bulwer. *The Complete Works of Edward Bulwer Lytton (Lord Lytton), Harold the Last of the Saxon Kings.* New York, NY: Lovell, Coryell & Co., no date.

Marietta Times. Marietta, OH: 1884-1887.

Mississippi, State of. *The Sword and Shield* and bibliographies. Archival Library, Jackson, MI, 1994.

National Archives. Veterans Pension Records, Henry S. Williams. General Reference Branch (NNRG-P). Washington D.C., 1994.

National Census. #470, August 23, 1850. Microfilm. 1850.

National Census. #148, June 8, 1860. Microfilm. 1860.

National Records, Brown County, Indiana. #187, CD Rom. Public Library, Marietta, OH, 1993.

Noble County Ohio Divorce and Marriage Records. Noble County Courthouse. Caldwell, OH.

O'Bryant, Michael, ed. *The Ohio Almanac.* Wilmington, Ohio: Orange Frazer Press, 1997.

Official Roster of the Soldiers of the State of Ohio in the War of the Rebellion, 1861-1866, vol V, 54th-69th Regiments-Infantry. Compiled under the directions of the Roster Commission. Akron, OH: The Werner Printing and Mfg. Co., 1887.

Paullin, Charles Oscar. *Atlas of Historical Geography of the United States.* Carnegie Institution of Washington and the American Geographical Society of New York, Publication No. 401. Baltimore, MD: A. Hoen & Co., Inc., 1932.

Pickenpaugh, Roger. *A History of Noble County.* Baltimore, MD: Gateway Press, Inc., 1988.

Potter, Jerry O. *The Sultana Tragedy, America's Greatest Maritime Disaster.* Gretna: Pelican Publishing Company, 1992.

Simpson, J. A. and E. S. C. Weiner. *The Oxford English Dictionary.* 2nd edition, vols V, VI, XI. Oxford, England: Clarendon Press, 1989.

Steinwehr, Adolph Wilhelm August Friedrich von, and Daniel Garrison Brinton. *Eclectic Series Intermediate Geography No. 2 with Lessons in Map Drawing.* Cincinnati, OH: Wilson Hinkle Co., 1870.

Trevorrow, Frank W. *Ohio's Canals - The Miami and Erie Canal,* 1973.

Vermont Historical Society. *Migration from Vermont 1716-1860.* Montpelier, VT: Vermont Historical Society, June vol V # 2, 1937.

Vezza, Dianne. Carrie Williams Lafferty Richardson. Advertisement bill, no date.

Washington County Ohio Census Records. 1839, 1840, 1850, 1860.

Washington County Marriage Records, vol 3. Washington County Courthouse, Marietta, OH. 1855 - 1865.

Way, Frederick, compiler. *Way's Pocket Directory* 1848-1983. Athens, OH: Ohio University Press. 1983.

Wheeler, Richard. *Voices of the Civil War.* New York, NY: Thomas Y. Crowell Company, 1976.

Williams, H.Z. *History of Washington County, Ohio: 1788-1881.* H. Z. Williams & Bro Publisher, 1881.

EDITOR'S NOTE

The small town of Marietta is no longer visited by presidents, kings, generals, and international novelists. Yet, buried deep in her soil are the roots of the people who colonized the West. From this area of Ohio, families and individuals spread into the wilderness to populate the states of Indiana, Illinois, Michigan, Iowa, Nebraska, Kansas, Oregon, and California. Some stayed but a short time in Washington County or the adjoining counties of Athens, Morgan, Monroe, and Noble, while others, like my grandfather, Adam Henry Young, born and reared here, chose to go West. At the age of eighteen he left Ohio for Enterprize, Oregon.

The Iroquois named the Ohio River "O-he-yo," which meant great river (O'Bryant 40). The great Ohio River encouraged early migration to this area. Upon its waters, people, animals, and possessions moved comfortably and effortlessly to the confluence of the Ohio and Muskingum Rivers at Marietta, or continued South and West into the Missouri and Mississippi river valleys.

While researching family genealogy, some of you may find your ancestors can be traced to the small, exquisite community of Marietta or to nearby farms and villages. It is entirely possible one of your ancestors knew this poet, read her poetry, and sang her songs.